Trade Credit and Risk Management

Trade Credit and Risk Management

Lucia Gibilaro

BEP BUSINESS EXPERT PRESS

First published in 2019 by
Business Expert Press, LLC
222 East 46th Street, New York, NY 10017
www.businessexpertpress.com

ISBN-13: 978-1-94944-325-7 (paperback)
ISBN-13: 978-1-94944-326-4 (e-book)

Business Expert Press Finance and Financial Management Collection

Collection ISSN: 2331-0049 (print)
Collection ISSN: 2331-0057 (electronic)

Cover and interior design by S4Carlisle Publishing Services Private Ltd., Chennai, India

First edition: 2019

10 9 8 7 6 5 4 3 2 1

Printed in the United States of America.

Dedication

What is essential is invisible to the eyes.

(de Saint-Exupéry A., 1943)

Abstract

Trade credit finance is characterized by strong attractiveness deriving from risk mitigation, but the plurality of sources of credit risk (default and dilution risk) requires the implementation of a credit risk management system that exploits the broad knowledge developed by financing supply relationships. Consequently, financiers could be hindered from developing a full understanding of the underwritten risks and are thus unable or only partially able to evaluate their full potential to expand financial relationships over the credit capability of a single counterparty with respect to the supplier–debtor pair. The richness of the information available in trade credit financing is not an obstacle for the development of a modern risk management framework, but it must be calibrated to avoid distortions in the implementation. In addition, risk analysis in the supply chain is not limited to the crises of individual members but must assess the effects of such crisis on the entire supply chain and assess the specific risks of contagion and the favorable conditions for the propagation. This book offers managers a complete analysis of the various issues of credit risk management for trade credit financing instruments supported by applications to various types of markets and presents an analysis on risks associated with trade credit in supply chains.

Keywords

credit risk; supply chain; trade credit

Brief Contents

Contents

Introduction

Trade credit is now extensively used in both international and domestic transactions in developed and developing countries. Therefore, the financing of trade credit is still a requirement for enterprises and an area for the development of market offers. The range of solutions to finance trade credit is fairly diversified, spanning from offers by financial intermediaries to markets, with a very interesting set of intermediate solutions arising from the application of new technologies to financial services; therefore, it is very important to delve into the motivations of the interest, in particular, of new providers. A distinctive role for financiers can be identified in the credit risk mitigation determined by trade credit such that more recent financing solutions based on crowdlending have enabled retail investors' investment in trade credits (Zhang et al. 2016). Moreover, the Basel Capital Accords include trade credit financing among risk-mitigated exposures (Basel Committee on Banking Supervision 2004). Despite acknowledgment of the credit risk mitigation associated with trade credit for financiers, empirical analysis of the conditions under which such mitigation can be effective is limited and, moreover, an indistinct approach is privileged. Consequently, financiers could be hindered from developing a full understanding of the underwritten risks and are thus unable or only partially able to evaluate their full potential to expand financial relationships over the credit capability of a single counterparty with respect to the supplier–debtor pair, as well as the supply chain to which they belong. Such shifts in risk evaluation are associated with change from a trade credit asset approach to a supply chain relationship approach. Therefore, the evaluation approach does not depend on the institutional classification of the trade credit financier and/or the technology applied but, instead, on the features of trade credit origination, which can be understood only by overcoming the limitations of the analysis based on each existing or future counterparties. The impact of such a shift can be particularly important in light of the support that trade credit provides in the economic growth of developing countries (Fisman and Love 2003) and the share of trade credit in the total assets of medium-sized enterprises in select sectors in developed countries (Carbo Valverde, Rodriguez Fernandez, and Udell 2016).

The research question on risk mitigation is associated with a more complex credit risk evaluation framework. Trade credit financiers evaluate the preexisting characteristics of trade credit and/or supply chain relationships and only then they financially intervene in such a relationship. Consequently, risk exposure depends on the trade credit financier's intervention in facilitating business relationships, while little impact can be exerted on the origination of the relationship. Regardless of the financial instrument selected, the trade credit financier's intervention can take the form of the advancement of credits and/or risk guarantee. Such complexity is not an obstacle in covering the richness of the information inside a modern risk management framework, but it must be calibrated to avoid distortions in implementation. Hence, internal rating systems must be tailored to generate output that is useful among a variety of internal processes.

Within the credit risk management framework, risk measurement at the individual level must address all material sources of losses and be consistent with managerial approaches. The inclusion of supply chain relationships within the credit risk management framework is associated with an increase in potential causes of losses due to dilution risk; therefore, trade credit financing requires an accurate assessment of the capacity of the capital buffer and risk frequency. A particularly relevant issue is the definition of the default status based on past due observations: The great frequency and breadth of business relationships from which financial intermediaries can observe debtor payment behavior must be exploited to gain greater insight. At the portfolio level, the measurement of concentration must be properly handled for greater capital allocation in front of excessive concentration at the sectorial and geographical levels, since concentration measures are associated with moderate losses in trade credit financing. Lastly, risk mitigation as determined by trade credit at both the individual and portfolio levels should consider potential contagion along the supply chain (Boissay and Gropp 2013), starting with the distinctive features of relationships that can affect the spread of distress from one member to the others. These research questions are particularly relevant in light of the evolution of prudential regulation on large exposures for financial intermediaries and the need to preserve the structure of supply chain relationships.

The research in this book addresses risk mitigation for trade credit financiers in a global context.

Based on the credit risk sources for trade credit financing, namely default risk, that is, the state of insolvency of the counterparty obliged to repay the exposure, and dilution risk, that is, the possibility that the receivable amount is reduced through cash or noncash credits to the receivable's obligor, Chapter 1 develops a credit risk management system. Starting with the design of an internal rating system, the chapter proposes complete implementation of the phases of credit risk evaluation and measurement at both the individual and portfolio levels. The analysis is accompanied by empirical evidence collected by trade credit financiers operating in different countries.

To achieve effective risk governance, risk measures must be embedded in the internal processes of financiers. Chapter 2, therefore, discusses calibrated implementation in the origination, control, and management of credit risk.

Since the risk mitigation ability of trade credits is acknowledged in the Basel Capital Accords, Chapter 3 focuses on the regulatory treatment of exposure to trade credit financing. When explicit references are not made by regulation, an effort is made to identify the application of prudential rules intended for universal and diversified banks. In summary, trade credits qualify for a wide range of options for determining minimum capital requirements. Further, the chapter analyzes the application of the large exposure standards in trade credit financing.

Finally, Chapter 4 focuses on contagion, an issue relevant to the risk-mitigating role attributed to trade credits, by delving into the distress that can spread among connected counterparties along the supply chain. An original empirical analysis is presented for the United States with the aim of evaluating characteristics affecting the impact of the distress of one member on others through the informative content of trade credit and support of growth. In particular, original insight is offered on the differences between the distress of a supplier with respect to the distress of a customer.

CHAPTER 1

Risk Management for Trade Credit Financing Instruments

Introduction

The risk mitigation of trade credits reflects the implementation of the credit risk management system by ensuring the convergence between the underlying risk exposure and the capital planning of the financiers. Given equal trade credits, exposure to credit risk depends on the legal characteristics of the transaction and the services offered, while risk mitigation depends on the credit risk embedded in the assets. Therefore, alternatives to the implementation of an internal rating system distinguish between exposures based on purchased and/or assigned trade receivables (see An Internal Rating System for Exposures Based on Purchased/Assigned Trade Receivables section) and exposures backed by trade receivables (see An Internal Rating System for Exposures Backed by Trade Receivables section). Once the conceptual framework for the implementation of the internal rating system is defined (see An Internal Rating System for Trade Credit Financing Instruments section), the specific characteristics of the lending activity require adaptations in the application of the standard credit risk measurement parameters at both the individual level (see Credit Risk Parameters: Theoretical Features and Empirical Evidence section) and portfolio level (see Concentration Risk: Alternative Approaches and Empirical Evidence section). Concluding remarks are presented in Conclusions section.

Trade Credit Financing and Credit Risk Exposure

The potential loss that a financier can incur in lending to a defaulted debtor is determined by the exposure to credit risk. Therefore, credit risk models must provide consistent estimations (Crouhy, Galai, and Mark 2000). Exposure to credit risk depends on the types of products (Araten and Jacobs 2001), and predictability is strictly affected by the relevance of the undrawn amount of the commitment (Asarnow and Marker 1995).

In trade credit financing, the origination of the exposure to credit risk must be carefully evaluated in light of the combination of the services offered to counterparties (Table 1.1). In transactions with recourse to the seller/assignor, trade credit financing determines an exposure to credit risk due to the on-balance sheet exposure deriving from the amount of the advance provided to the seller/assignor or the total price paid for purchasing the receivables. In the absence of disbursement by the financier, any exposure to credit risk is outlined. Regarding transactions without recourse, the exposure to credit risk originates from the outstanding amount of trade credits assigned/purchased, regardless of any cash exposure stemming from the provision of an advance or payment of the purchasing price. The financier has made a commitment to guarantee the seller/assignor for the default of trade debtors. Therefore, even though only part of the commitment has already been provided, the residual part of the receivables assigned/purchased will be due according to the agreed terms and conditions. Therefore, in light of multiple sources affecting credit risk, cash exposure is relevant only to measure credit exposure due to dilution risk.[1]

Table 1.1 Trade credit financing services and the exposure to credit risk

	With on-balance sheet exposure	Without on-balance sheet exposure
With recourse	Credit risk determined by the advance/purchasing price	No credit risk
Without recourse	Credit risk determined by the commitment to guarantee for trade debtors default	Credit risk determined by the commitment to guarantee for trade debtors default

Source: Author's elaborations.

---

[1] See An Internal Rating System for Exposures Backed by Trade Receivables section.

The classification of exposures to credit risk in combination with services offered presented in Table 1.1 must be considered from a dynamic perspective. Because trade credit financing has a revolving nature, transactions that do not currently involve exposures to credit risk can become risky because of approbation in credit limits deliberated by the financier.

An Internal Rating System for Trade Credit Financing Instruments

Modern credit risk management is based on the development of credit risk models encompassing all policies, procedures, and practices used by a financial intermediary in estimating a credit portfolio's probability density function (Basel Committee on Banking Supervision 1999). Estimation of the probability density function of potential losses requires the implementation of an internal rating system that comprises all the methods, processes, controls, and data collection and information technology systems that support the assessment of credit risk through the assignment of internal risk ratings and the quantification of default and losses estimates (Basel Committee on Banking Supervision 2004).

Even though a flourishing academic and professional literature on internal rating systems has emerged, their implementation for trade credit financing exposure still has issues to be resolved due to the specific characteristics of the lending activity. In particular, because risk management is intended to ensure the integrated control of risks to allocate capital efficiently (Saita 1999) and the ratings to be assumed as risk proxies must produce a reliable evaluation (Nocco and Stulz 2006) of the potential losses for each exposure, internal rating systems are found that refer to both the borrower and the facility (Foglia, Iannotti, and Marullo Reedtz 2001). Since trade credit financing exposures are involved, the alignment between risk measures and underlying risks requires the development of a facility-oriented internal rating system. Because of the self-liquidating nature of the exposure, the rating assignment must evaluate the risk of the relationship between the supplier and the customer consistently with the risk taken on by the financier (Figure 1.1).

```
        ┌─────────────────────────┐
        │   Credit risk evaluation │
        │      of the exposure     │
        └─────────────────────────┘
```

| Default risk | | Dilution risk |

| Rating of exposures based on purchased/assigned trade receivables | Rating of exposures backed by trade receivables |

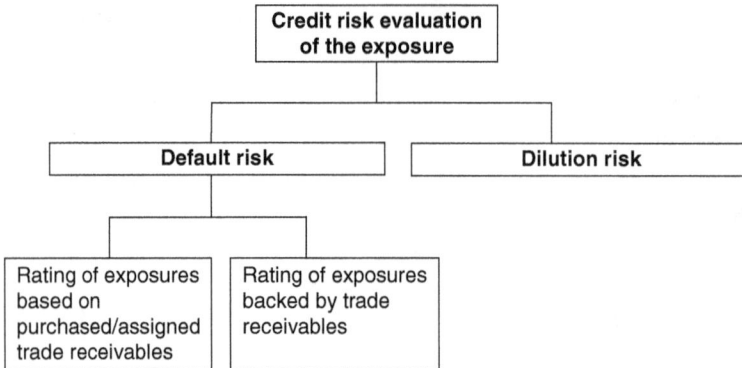

Figure 1.1 Credit risk evaluation of trade credit financing exposures

Source: Author's elaboration.

In light of the multiple sources that can determine credit losses in trade credit financing, the internal rating system must obtain a credit rating for the exposure based on the synthesis of

- Default risk
- Dilution risk

The implementation of the default risk rating for trade credit financing is based on management activity. The management of receivables provides the lender information unavailable in transactions where receivables back the loans provided to the seller/assignor. The planning of the system is articulated in two segments:

- The rating of exposures based on purchased/assigned trade receivables. All exposures characterized by managed receivables are rated in this segment, even under undisclosed assignments.
- The rating of exposures backed by trade receivables. Receivables mitigate a financier's risk through collateralization; assignments of future credits are rated in this segment.

Regardless of the default risk segment, the rating system is characterized by two dimensions depicting the risk of loss (Figure 1.2). For each

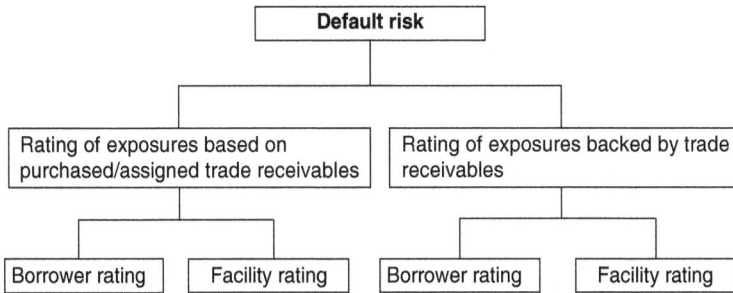

*Figure 1.2 Rating system for the default risk of trade credit financing
exposure*

Source: Author's elaboration.

exposure, the dimensions associated with the relevant risk parameters are
as follows (Crouhy, Galai, and Mark 2001):

- The borrower rating, which determines the probability of the obligor's default (*PD*);
- The facility rating, which determines the loss parameters in the
  case of the obligor's default, that is, the loss given default (*LGD*),
  exposure at default (*EAD*), and maturity (*M*).

The evaluation of dilution risk concerns only ordinary dilution. Consistent with the classification of causes (Gibilaro 2006a), exceptional dilution will be assessed in both the aforementioned default risk system and
the operational risk system. The internal assessment of dilution risk is
associated with a risk parameter expressed in terms of the expected loss
rate (ELR_d).

An Internal Rating System for Exposures Based on Purchased/ Assigned Trade Receivables

The conceptual framework of the internal rating system for exposures
based on purchased/assigned trade receivables requires a combination
of many risk factors to obtain both the borrower and facility ratings
(Figure 1.3).

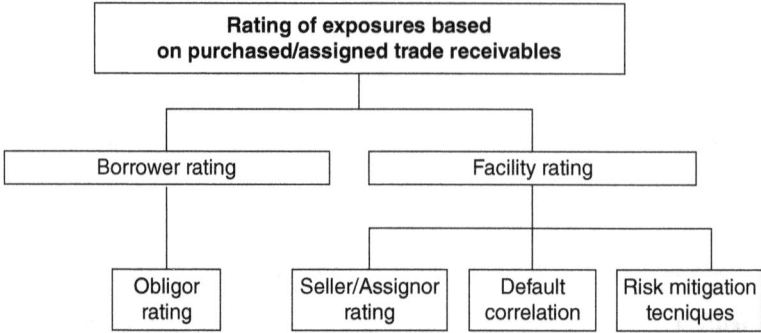

Figure 1.3 Internal rating system for exposures based on purchased/ assigned trade receivables

Source: Author's elaboration.

The borrower rating is based on the obligor's creditworthiness. The counterparty borrowing money is not the counterparty obliged to pay back the advance. The potential market segments of trade debtors are rather diversified: The exposure to different market segments is not the choice of the financier but, rather, originates from the matching between the type of supply and the type of buyer (see Figure 1.4).

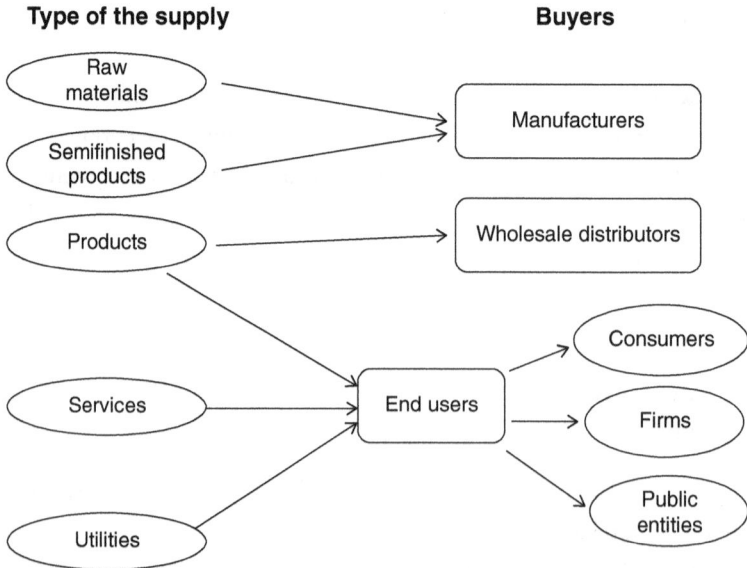

Figure 1.4 Matching of the type of supply and the type of buyer

Source: Author's elaboration.

Even though financiers can develop their own segmentation, starting with the matching of the type of supply and borrower, trade credit financing exposures can be classified according to standard approaches for segmenting financial exposures:

A) Domestic
  1. Large corporations and corporations. According to prudential regulatory provisions, this segment should group entities with a turnover totaling over 50 million euros (Basel Committee on Banking Supervision 2004), while corporations under this threshold belong to the middle market (Ughetto 2008).
  2. Small- and medium-sized enterprises (SMEs). Inside this segment, empirical evidence shows distinct risk profile characteristics (Dietch and Petey 2004):
     - Very small SMEs, with a turnover between 0.15 million euros and 1 million euros
     - Medium SMEs, with a turnover between 1 million euros and 7 million euros
     - Large SMEs, with a turnover between 7 million euros and 40 million euros
  3. Central and noncentral public entities
  4. Consumers
B) Foreign
  1. Large corporate and corporate
  2. SMEs
  3. Central and local public entities

Depending on the size of the obligor (Tschemernjak 2004), financiers can adopt the following approaches for the rating attribution (Bielecki, Crepey, and Jeanblanc 2010):

  • Bottom-up approach. This approach is suitable for counterparties who can determine potential relevant losses for the financier and for which individual information is available to assess the obligor's risk characteristics. This approach is appropriate for large and other corporate entities as well as central and noncentral public entities, whereas for SMEs, the choice depends on the relative importance of the counterparty in the financier's balance sheet.

- Top-down approach. Debtors associated with limited potential losses are assessed according to the homogeneous group to which they belong. Therefore, the output reflects the average risk of the pool rather than the specific creditworthiness of each obligor. The approach is less time-consuming than the previous approach, but the decomposition of expected risk into risk factors is not feasible. This approach is appropriate for SME entities and consumers.

Once the obligor is rated, the facility rating requires the rating attribution of the seller/assignor of trade receivables. Compared with trade debtors, the potential segments of seller/assignors are limited to the following categories:

A) Domestic
   1. Large corporations and corporations
   2. SMEs
B) Foreign large corporations and corporations

The approach for rating the seller/assignor is mainly bottom-up due to the relevance of the counterparty (Ruozi and Rossignoli 1985), with which multiple trade debtors are generally associated (Van Horen 2007). Only when reverse factoring is considered is the top-down approach suitable for sellers/assignors, due to the limited size of the former relative to trade debtors.

Initially, the facility rating of exposures based on purchased trade receivables can benefit from recourse to the seller/assignor if the debtor has defaulted. The effectiveness of this risk mitigation depends on the correlation between the default risk of the seller/assignor and that of the trade debtor. Generally, the correlation depends on systemic factors causing defaults to cluster and is critical in the estimation of extreme credit losses (Cowan and Cowan 2004). Factors linking firms' health are not limited to systemic ones. Therefore, default correlation analysis must also consider semispecific factors, such as the industry and geographical area (Lucas 1995). Because the guarantee provided by the seller/assignor arises from a preexisting commercial transaction, the assessment of default correlation must also consider specific factors, because of the supply chain relationship between the counterparties. The ability of the counterparties to be correlated in their entry into default status is not insignificant (Wagner and Bode 2011) and can also arise from contagion along the supply chain (Zhang and Li 2010). Therefore, the risk mitigation determined by recourse to the seller/assignor should be evaluated in light of the risk of the supplier relationship (Hallikas et al. 2005). The drivers of the vulnerability of the supply chain relationship are as follows (Wagner and Bode 2006):

- Supplier dependence, that is, the extent to which the customer sources inputs from a supplier for which there are few alternative sources, as well as the mutuality of the relationship.
- The supplier's concentration in the market, which can prevent firms from switching vendors given supplier disruption.
- Global sourcing, which can increase the complexity of the supply chain. Nonetheless, it must be recognized that global sourcing can allow for the diversification of risk factors affecting the supplier and the buyer (Babich, Burnetas, and Ritchken 2007).

The effectiveness of the risk mitigation deriving from recourse to the seller/assignor is particularly important to ex ante high-risk trade debtors, since suppliers maintain trade relationships under the following conditions (Garcia-Appendini and Montoriol-Garriga 2015):

- The client has a large concentration of sales.
- The supplier sells a large portion of its products to the distressed client.
- The supplier sells differentiated goods to the distressed clients.
- The client is located close to the supplier's headquarters.

Risk mitigation techniques play a central role in the credit risk management framework (Altman 2002). Trade credit insurance is a prominent instrument in ensuring resilient supply relationships for suppliers and complementing trade credit financing instruments (Jones 2010), suitable in both domestic and international supply chain relationships.

In the management of firms and financial intermediaries, credit insurance represents an alternate accounts receivable policy (Mian and Smith 1992). Generally, trade credit insurance covers a portfolio of buyers by outsourcing the potential losses determined by the counterparty's default. Standard trade credit insurance covers all receivables, while specific contracts can apply to specific customers or transactions (Riestra 2003).

Frequently, the risk transfer is partial, due to clauses addressing information asymmetry issues (Sokolovska 2017) such as the following:

- Deductibles, that is, limits whereby a loss has to exceed an agreed threshold before a claim can be submitted to the insurer, or the insured supplier will assume this first level of loss for its own account.
- Limits, where each buyer is granted a specific credit limit up to which the financier's exposure is granted. Limits can also refer to the entire portfolio.
- Excess loss, that is, the insurer covers only the excess of losses with respect to a long-term statistic; that is, the clause can be negotiated for large companies being insured.

Trade credit insurance is found multiplying exports with respect to covered exports (Van der Veer 2015). The risk mitigated by the financier covers nonpayment deriving from either commercial or political risk. Insurance contracts are for both the short- and medium–long term and the involvement of governments is relevant at the global level due to the support of international sales (Funatsu 1986).

As for other financial exposures, trade credit financiers can mitigate default risk through personal guarantees, collaterals, and credit derivatives.[2]

An Internal Rating System for Exposures Backed by Trade Receivables

The implementation of an internal rating system for exposures backed by trade receivables is bidimensional, based on the characteristics of the borrower and the facility rating (Figure 1.5).

---

[2]For a broader discussion on credit risk transfer instruments, see Kiff, Michaud, and Mitchell (2003).

```
┌─────────────────────────────────────────────────────┐
│  Rating of exposures backed by trade receivables      │
└─────────────────────────────────────────────────────┘
            │                             │
   ┌─────────────────┐           ┌─────────────────┐
   │  Borrower rating │           │  Facility rating │
   └─────────────────┘           └─────────────────┘
            │                   │          │          │
   ┌─────────────┐    ┌────────────┐ ┌───────────┐ ┌─────────────┐
   │ Seller/Assignor│  │   Trade    │ │  Default  │ │Risk mitigation│
   │    rating      │  │ receivables│ │correlation│ │  tecniques  │
   └─────────────┘    └────────────┘ └───────────┘ └─────────────┘
```

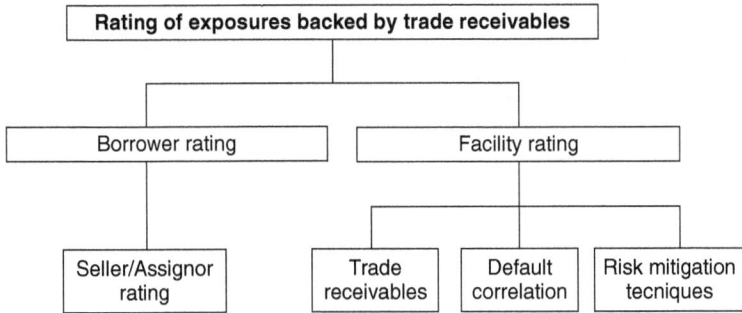

Figure 1.5 Internal rating system for exposures backed by trade receivables

Source: Author's elaboration.

The borrower rating is based on the creditworthiness of the seller/assignor: Better borrower ratings are associated with a lower expectation of entry into default status. The segmentation of the system reflects institutional sellers, which reduces to firms selling output to different types of buyers. Even though financiers can develop their own segmentation, according to standard approaches adopted by financial intermediaries, borrowers belong to the following segments:

A) Domestic
   1. Large corporations and corporations
   2. SMEs
B) Foreign
   1. Large corporations and corporations

Sellers/assignors should be treated under a bottom-up approach not only because each seller/assignor is matched with multiple buyers but also because the information set on the commercial relationship is limited due to the absence of receivables management. The importance of adopting a bottom-up approach for the seller/assignor is even more relevant for financial exposures stemming from future credits.

Initially, the facility rating is affected by the trade receivables backing the exposure to the seller/assignor, which excludes receivables from affiliates. Moreover, the financier must trust the borrower's credit policy to assume the receivables mitigate the exposure to the seller/assignor.

Because the receivables are not managed, a top-down approach can be developed to obtain a pool risk assessment. The ability of pools of trade receivables to mitigate risk depends on

- The correlation between the industries of the seller/assignor and the trade debtors
- The diversification of the trade debtors and the concentration of receivables

As in the internal rating system for purchased trade receivables, other credit risk transfer can be used by the financier. In particular, such credit risk mitigation pertains to the default risk of the seller/assignor.

Credit Risk Parameters: Theoretical Features and Empirical Evidence

Beyond producing the inputs for credit risk models, the applications of internal rating systems span many of the financier's activities (see Chapter 2). The use of internal ratings by other applications depends on the estimation of the credit risk parameters (Carey and Hrycay 2001) relevant in trade credit financing (PD, LGD, EAD, M, ELR_d). Estimation of the credit risk parameters is based on the following phases of the process (De Laurentis, Maino, and Molteni 2010):

- Rating assignment. This phase is intended to classify each borrower/facility into one of the grades/pools of the rating system.
- Rating quantification. During this phase, each rating grade/pool is associated with the expected values of the relevant credit risk parameter expressing the risk of each grade/pool.

Default Risk

Probability Default

The borrower rating reflects the creditworthiness of the counterparty and is associated with the counterparty's PD. Therefore, the internal rating system for trade credit financing exposures applies to

- The trade debtor
- The seller assignor
- The financial guarantor

The approaches to assign counterparties borrower rating grades differ according to the diversification of the segments describing the financier's counterparties. Therefore, the analysis must differ among corporate, retail, and public counterparties.

Regardless of the size of the corporate entities and the level of analysis, the assignment of counterparties to rating grades aims to predict creditworthiness, that is, the possibility of entry into default status, through the analysis of the following profiles addressing both financial and nonfinancial factors (Grunert, Norden, and Weber 2004):

- Economic, financial, and assets and liabilities statements. More than calculating the key ratios, such profile allows one to assess access to various financing sources from different lenders and the counterparty's repayment capability.
- The industry and position in the market. In particular, the analysis aims to examine the key drivers of market positioning, such as the business model, reputation and alliances, and supply chain membership.
- Management, organization, and governance. This profile allows one to evaluate the ability of management to reach goals, the coordination of resources, and the relationships between the entity and different stakeholders.

To assign rating grades to the counterparties, many sources must be considered together to analyze the relevant profiles. Even though each financier owns its specific rating process, the main information sources refer to the following (Caselli and Gatti 2003):

- The balance sheet. This represents the fundamental source for investigating economic, financial, and assets and liabilities statements.
- Credit registers and the monitoring process. These sources complement the balance sheet in focusing on the counterparty's financial profile by adding insight from existing financial relationships with both the financier and the entire financial system.

- Sectorial analysis. These reports allow the financier to determine the potential growth of the sector and opportunities and threats. By complementing the analysis with information on the firm's strengths and weaknesses, the business risk of the counterparty can be determined.
- Governance and investor relationship documentation. Even though the balance sheet contains reports of the relevant facts characterizing management activity, it is important to analyze the approaches taken to address outsider interests.
- A questionnaire and interviews. These sources allow one to determine information not contained in the previous types of documentation, with the aim of evidencing firm-specific characteristics relevant to broadening the insight of standardized information and to delve into nonstandardized information.

The relevance of the aforementioned profiles in the rating assignment process can improve the prediction of business failure. Nonfinancial information favors the stability of assignments over time (Brunner, Krahnen, and Weber 2000) and strong corporate governance fosters higher internal ratings (Ashbaugh-Skaife, Collins, and LaFond 2006). Nonetheless, one should note that SME exposures differ from corporate and large corporate exposures as follows (Rikkers and Thibeault 2007):

- Information. SME loans are illiquid and market data are not available. Moreover, accounting data are available only yearly and are characterized by unproven quality.
- Economy. SMEs are sensitive to the state of the economy and the impact of the business cycle can be strongly due to the absence of scale effects, limited market power, a modest learning effect, and a smaller output market.
- Cost. The relative size of each exposure and its potential losses are limited with respect to the financier. Therefore, a single loan cannot make a lender insolvent. Moreover, risk evaluation is time-consuming and financiers face fixed costs in such a process; therefore, evaluating SMEs is more expensive.

The information for evaluating the profiles assessed in the internal rating assignment is summarized in Table 1.2.

Table 1.2 Segment and critical information for rating assignment

Segment	Information source
Corporate and large corporate	• Balance sheet • Relationships with the financial system • Sectorial analysis • Questionnaire/interviews
SME	• Balance sheet • Relationships with the financial system • Sectorial analysis

Regardless of the firm's size, the internal ratings baseline is represented by the assessment of the financial profile. Over the years, many studies have investigated at the international level the relationship between financial variables and default to develop automated decision systems based on the attribution of a score to the counterparty (Capon 1982). The models vary by feature as follows (Altman and Narayanan 1997):

- Modeling techniques. Even though many techniques have been developed over time, multiple discriminant analysis continues to play a main role in empirical studies.
- Data. Information to implement models continues to represent an important issue in the validation of the results.
- Definition of default. The definition of default varies with the empirical analysis (i.e., bankruptcy filing by a company, bond default, bank loan default, delisting, government intervention via special financing, and liquidation), spanning from an internal definition to a judicial one, even though the accumulation of data after the implementation of Basel II Capital Accord should have favored the development of studies based on a common definition of default based on past dues.

Numerous studies (Table 1.3), based on both developed and developing countries, have been conducted around Altman's (1968) pioneering work. The recurring predictive variables in the models involve the following evaluation areas:

- Profitability
- Assets and liabilities

- Financial flows
- The market value of capital

For each valuation area, the selection of default risk indicator variables and their relevance differs according to the research, although common information can be identified to investigate certain profiles (Table 1.3). In the context of profitability, the models initially identify in the relation between turnover and total assets a prediction of default risk that reflects a potential development measure of the enterprise. Taking into account the cost structure, it is possible to underline the comparison with respect to operating profitability and leverage. Furthermore, the models show the share of profits in the remuneration of the invested capital. Taking into account areas other than the core business, the models identify both the interest coverage of the operating income and pretax profitability as predictors of the risk of insolvency. The company's growth prospects, identified in the reinvestment of earnings, predict the insolvency of the enterprise, and studies investigating enterprise development identify the rate of rotation of stocks as an effective predictor. Concerning assets and liabilities, prediction models identify a relation between the two and, moreover, the composition of stable external funds and their weight on the invested capital. From a short-term perspective, models identify the ratio of working capital to total wealth and/or to total debt as an important variable in predicting business failure. Looking at cash flows, the relations with external debt and sales are outlined as predictive by many studies. Moreover, quick assets are considered relevant in predicting business failure. By considering the last area, the market value of equity is found to be predictive when compared to the book value and to total liabilities.

Among surveyed predictive variables (Table 1.3), trade receivables and payables show, in studies based on multiple discriminant analysis, only indirectly through the contribution to working capital. Note that when other financial variables are omitted, different elements of the trade credit policy can predict business failure (Terradez et al. 2015). Such variables can be very useful for predicting the business failure of counterparties without balance sheet data, particularly in the case of SME.

Table 1.3 An international survey of scoring models for corporate entities

Author	Year	Model	Financial variables
Altman	1968	Multiple discriminant analysis	• working capital/total assets • retained earnings/total assets • Earnings before interest and taxes (EBIT)/total assets • market value of equity/book value of liabilities • sales/totaled assets
Weibel	1973	Univariate analysis	• liquidity (near monetary resource asset – current liabilities)/operating expenses prior to depreciation • inventory turnover • debt/assets
Taffler and Tisshaw	1977	Multiple discriminant analysis	• profit before taxes/current assets • current assets/total assets • current liabilities/total assets • credit interval:liquidity – current assets/operating costs
Altman, Baidya, and Ribeiro-Dias	1979	Multiple discriminant analysis	• retained earnings/assets • EBIT/assets • sales/assets • market value of equity/book value of liabilities
Bilderbeek	1979	Multiple discriminant analysis	• retained earnings/total assets • added value/total assets • trade payables/sales • sales/total assets • profit after taxes/equity
Marais Earl and Marais	1979 1982	Multiple discriminant analysis	• current assets/gross total assets • 1/gross total assets • cash flow/current liabilities • (funds generated from operations – net change in working capital)/debt
Takahashi, Kurokawa, and Watase	1979	Multiple discriminant analysis	• net worth/fixed assets • current liabilities/assets • voluntary reserves plus inappropriate surplus/assets • interest expense/sales • earned surplus • increase in residual value/sales • ordinary profit/assets sales – variable costs

(continued)

Table 1.3 Continued

Author	Year	Model	Financial variables
Altman and Lavallee	1981	Multiple discriminant analysis	• sales/total assets • total debt/total assets • current assets/current liabilities • net profit after tax/total debt • growth rate of equity – growth rate of asset
Altman and Izan Izan	1981 1984	Multiple discriminant analysis	• operating income/shareholder funds • EBIT/total assets • net profit after tax/total assets • cash flow/financial debt • current assets/current liabilities • inventories/current liabilities-overdrafts • funded debt/shareholders funds • market value of equity/total liabilities • book value of liabilities/market value of equity
Taffler	1982	Principal component analysis	• profit before taxes/total assets • total liabilities/fixed assets • quick assets/total assets • working capital/ net worth • turnover of inventories
Ko	1982	Multiple discriminant analysis	• EBIT/sales • turnover of inventories 2 years before default/ turnover of inventories 3 years before default • standard error of net profit (years) • working capital/total debt • market value of equity/total debt
Ta and Seah	1988	Multiple discriminant analysis	• operating profit/liabilities • current assets/current liabilities • EBIT/paid-up capital • sales/working capital • (current assets – stocks – current liabilities)/EBIT • total shareholders' fund/ liabilities • ordinary shareholders' fund/ capital used

Table 1.3 Continued

Author	Year	Model	Financial variables
Baetge, Huss, and Niehaus	1988	Multiple discriminant analysis	• net worth/(total assets – quick assets – property and plant) • (operating income + ordinary depreciation + addition to pension reserves)/assets • (cash income – expenses)/short-term liabilities
Bhatia	1988	Multiple discriminant analysis	• cash flow/debt • current ratio • profit after tax/net worth • interest/output • sales/assets • stock of finished goods/sales • working capital management ratio
Fernandez	1988	Multiple discriminant analysis	• return on investment • cash flow/current liabilities • quick ratio/industry value • before tax earnings/sales • cash flow/sales • (permanent funds/net fixed assets)/industry value
Gloubos and Grammatikos	1988	• Linear probit model • Probit analysis • Logit analysis • Linear discriminant analysis	• gross income/current liabilities • debt/assets • net working capital/assets • gross income/assets • current assets/current liabilities
Pascale	1988	Multiple discriminant analysis	• sales/debt • net earnings/assets • long-term debt/total debt
Suominen	1988	Multinomial logit model	• profitability:(quick flow – direct taxes)/assets • liquidity:(quick assets/total assets) • liabilities/asset
Unal	1988	Multiple discriminant analysis	• EBIT/assets • quick assets/current debt • net working capital/sales • quick assets/inventory • debt/assets • long-term debt/assets

Table 1.3 Continued

Author	Year	Model	Financial variables
Altman, Marco, and Varetto	1994	Linear discriminant analysis and neural networks	• ability to bear cost of debt • liquidity • ability to bear financial debt • profitability • assets/liabilities • profit accumulation • trade indebtedness • efficiency
Von Stein and Ziegler	1984	Nonparametric and parametric methods	• capital borrowed/total capital • short-term borrowed capital/ output • accounts payable for purchases and deliveries/material costs • (bill of exchange liabilities + accounts payable)/output • (current assets – short-term borrowed capital)/output • equity/(total assets – liquid assets – real estate) • equity/(tangible property – real estate) • short-term borrowed capital/ current assets • (working expenditure – depreciation on tangible property)/(liquid assets + accounts receivable – short-term borrowed capital) • operational result/capital • (operational result + depreciation)/net turnover; (operational result + depreciation)/ short-term borrowed capital • (operational result + depreciation)/total capital borrowed
Altman, Kim, and Eom	1995	Multiple discriminant analysis	• log(assets) • log(sales/assets) • retained earnings/assets • market value of equity/ liabilities
Terradez, Kizys, Juan, Debon, and Sawik	2015	Multivariate decision tree model	• account receivables/total assets • account payables/total liabilities • account payables growth • account receivables growth • days accounts payable • days accounts receivable

Source: Author's elaboration.

Although the discussion above considers a rating assignment using information on each counterparty, the rating assignment can also follow a top-down approach (see An Internal Rating System for Trade Credit Financing Instruments section). In particular, pools of trade debtors can be formed according to the following:

- Relevant seller/assignor. For n assignor/sellers, $n \times n$ pools can be formed. This criterion can drive pool origination when a financier buys trade credits mainly based on the average quality of the receivables and the risk and reputation of the seller/assignor (Sopranzetti 1998).
- Sectorial activity of the seller/assignor. Pools are segmented by the activity of the seller/assignor, regardless of the customer segment. This criterion is adopted particularly in trade credit financing transactions characterized by delegation of the management activity to the seller/assignors (Palia and Sopranzetti 2004).
- Product. Trade credits are grouped according to the financier's offer, regardless of the pair that originated the receivable (Dionne and Harchaoui 2008).
- Type of trade debtor. According to this criterion, the pools' origination is not affected by seller/assignor characteristics or, more generally, by the supply relationship. The credit quality of the trade debtor guides pool formation, regardless of recourse to the seller/assignor (Ernst & Young 2016).

The top-down approach is widely applied in trade credits to consumers that originated from relationships with either retailers or utilities companies/public sector entities. Although the fine granularity of the portfolio ensures an individual's limited exposure, covariance risk cannot be considered insignificant. Therefore, the following criteria can be adopted in pool creation (Reuter 2006):

- Age
- Family status
- Income
- Marital status

- Real estate ownership/rental status
- Geographical area
- Revolving contract

The last market segment of potential trade debtors is represented by central and local public administration entities. The opportunity to propose standard approaches is strongly affected by the different cash flow profiles due to different regimes in imposing and collecting taxes at the central, local, and cross-border levels. Nonetheless, it can be useful to examine the criteria developed by rating agencies to assess the risk of non-reimbursement and/or nonpayment of interest on a financial debt, considering both the solicited and—when unavailable—unsolicited versions, since these criteria are reliable in the funding of sovereign, state, and municipal entities. The rating assignments of sovereign entities are based on numerous social, political, and economic factors, including the following quantitative determinants (Cantor and Packer 1996):

- Per capita income
- Gross domestic product (GDP) growth
- Inflation
- Fiscal balance
- External balance
- External debt
- Economic development
- Default history

At the subsovereign level, a state's risk of default is determined mainly by its financial profile linked to its net revenue generation capability, based on the sources it can activate to produce taxes and the volume of existing debt. In particular, the following are relevant variables (Pu and Thakor 1984):

- The state's existing debt, including
  - Total net direct debt burden
  - Ratio of total net direct debt to total taxable property in the state

- ○ Ratio of total net direct debt to total personal income
- ○ Per capita debt
- The state's tax revenue sources, including
  - ○ Unemployment rate
  - ○ Population
  - ○ Population change over 5 years
  - ○ Median family income
  - ○ Median home value
  - ○ Per capita personal income

The rating assigned to a state is relevant to the rating assigned to its municipalities, with a positive impact on the final assessment (Capeci 1991). Generally, the rating of a municipality is a function of the following (Hàjek 2011):

- Economic and socioeconomic factors. The relevant variables are the population, population growth, the median family income, and the unemployment rate.
- Debt, including size and structure. This factor is proxied by the following variables:
  - ○ Debt service to total revenue
  - ○ Total debt to population
  - ○ Long-term debt to population
- Budget implementation. Investigation of this factor is based on financial variables such as
  - ○ Debt service to total revenue
  - ○ Total debt to population
  - ○ Total revenue to population
  - ○ Current revenues to current expenditures
  - ○ Tax collectibles to population
  - ○ General revenues accounted for by intergovernmental grants
- Administrative characteristics. Obviously, the relevant variables are both
  - ○ Qualitative, covering the entity's organization, human capital, and strategy
  - ○ Quantitative, dealing prevalently with the tax collection rate and standardized forms of government

In conclusion on the topic of the public administration portfolio, it is to be remembered that the creditworthiness of the entity evaluated through the aforementioned criteria adopted by rating agencies cannot mirror the effective risk taken on by the trade credit financier, for the following reasons:

- Trade credits originated by the suppliers of public administration are sometimes subject to conditions rather than payment terms. A trade credit can be considered due only upon completion of administrative verification and settlement procedures imposed by law for the protection of public interests and the verification of the absence of legal impossibility for the entity to proceed with the payment due. Moreover, firm trade credits deriving from direct and indirect taxes are characterized by a minimum term before they become due, but a maximum term if the payment is not fixed.
- More than relying on creditworthiness, repayment capability depends on the process of spending and transferring funds between central and local entities and the effectiveness of tax and collection activities at the local level.

After the discussion of approaches to assigning a rating grade to the counterparties involved in trade credit financing, the following step address the rating quantification of default probabilities where, if the discrete form is adopted, are estimated over a one-year horizon (Bessis 2015). The characteristics of this phase concern

A) The definition of default
B) The approach to quantify the PD associated with the different grades

Consistent with the general goal of risk management to allocate capital efficiently, the definition of default must be sufficiently predictive of the default status to preserve the bank's capital. The importance of this choice follows from the impact of the definition on the predictive variables (Lin, Ansell, and Adreeva 2012).

In light of the introduction and the broad international adoption of prudential standards, the implementation of internal rating systems has been increasingly based on the Basel II Capital Accord definition of default. According to prudential regulation, a counterparty is classified defaulted under the following conditions (Basel Committee on Banking Supervision 2006):

- The financier considers that the obligor is unlikely to pay its credit obligations to the group in full, without recourse to actions such as realizing security (if held).
- The obligor is more than 90 days past due on any material credit obligation to the group. Overdrafts will be considered past due once the customer has breached an advised limit or been advised of a limit smaller than the current outstanding.

The following elements indicate unlikeliness to pay:

- The financier gives the credit obligation a nonaccrual status.
- The financier writes a charge-off or account-specific provision resulting from a significant perceived decline in credit quality subsequent to the bank taking on the exposure.
- The financier sells the credit obligation at a material credit-related economic loss.
- The financier consents to a distressed restructuring of the credit obligation that is likely to result in a diminished financial obligation caused by the material forgiveness or postponement of principal, interest, or (where relevant) fees.
- The financier has filed for the obligor's bankruptcy or a similar order due to the obligor's credit obligation to the banking group.
- The obligor has sought or has been placed in bankruptcy or similar protection that would avoid or delay repayment of the credit obligation.

The different events quoted by the Basel II Capital Accord span from high, prudent classifications to the legal certainty of the default status (Figure 1.6).

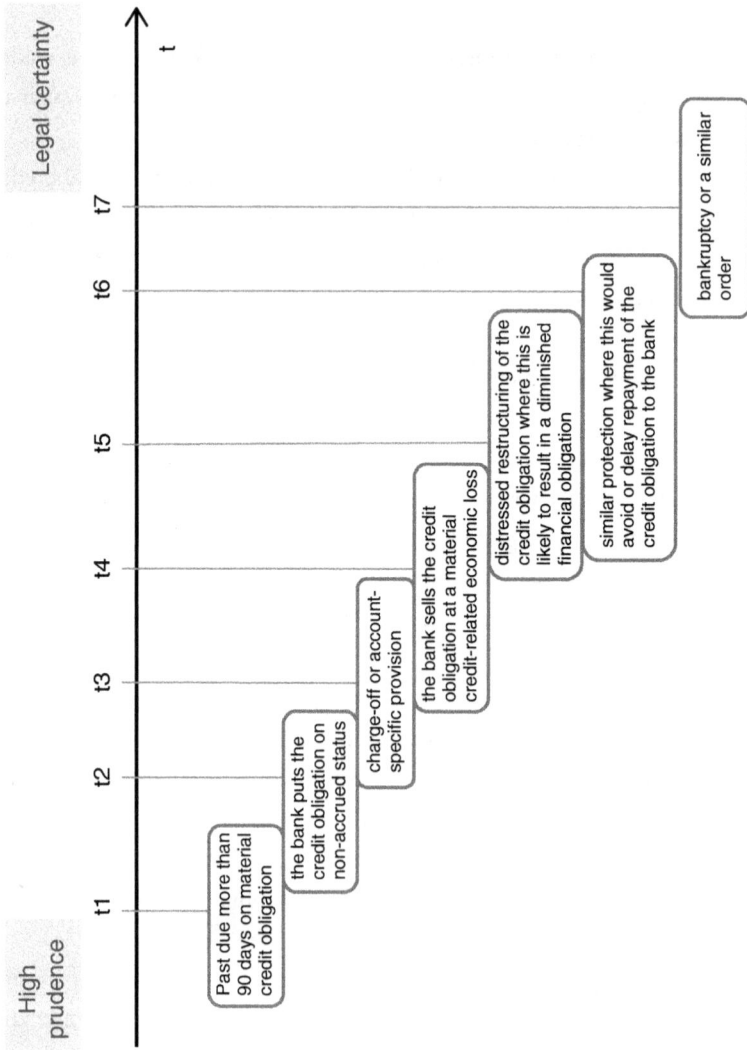

High prudence

Legal certainty

t1 — Past due more than 90 days on material credit obligation

t2 — the bank puts the credit obligation on non-accrued status

t3 — charge-off or account-specific provision

t4 — the bank sells the credit obligation at a material credit-related economic loss

t5 — distressed restructuring of the credit obligation where this is likely to result in a diminished financial obligation

t6 — similar protection where this would avoid or delay repayment of the credit obligation to the bank

t7 — bankruptcy or a similar order

Figure 1.6 *Definition of default under the Basel II Capital Accord*

Source: Author's elaboration.

Because trade credit financing exposures are characterized by potential delinquency events (Gibilaro, 2006a), a counterparty can enter into default as defined by 90 days past due, but without subsequently evolving toward the legal certainty of the default status. In light of international payment practices in commercial transactions, this situation is not unusual (Figure 1.7): All countries show a positive percentage of payments exceeding 90 days among total payments. All else being equal, smaller entities are characterized by a higher share of payments past 90 days. Moreover, the distribution of such payments is affected by geographical area, showing higher distributions for Asian, Mediterranean, and Eastern European countries.

To moderate the risk of the adoption of a default definition on the counterparty's payment history also encompassing temporary illiquidity situations, Basel II recommendations specify that only material 90 days past dues can trigger the default classification. In the absence of a prescription for the materiality threshold, diversified choices are adopted at the international level. The solutions implemented show that the materiality threshold can be expressed as follows (European Banking Authority 2016):

- A hard limit. The threshold can be either an absolute or a relative term. In the first case, percentages range from 1 to 10 percent and absolute values can reach 50,000 euros.
- A soft limit. Financiers can establish their own materiality thresholds or adopt a case-by-case approach.

Regardless of the quantitative level of the threshold, payment practices are strongly affected by the type of sector. Payment practices differ among economic sectors and, on average, tend to be longer in construction, transportation and distribution, and retail (Figure 1.8).

Payment delays are important in the public sector. Effective payment periods are longer than 90 days in the Euro-Mediterranean countries but significant gaps in commercial payments by the public sector are observed for most of the surveyed countries (Figure 1.9).

Figures 1.7 to 1.9 show that payment habits cluster by sector and geographical area. Therefore, the application of common thresholds can

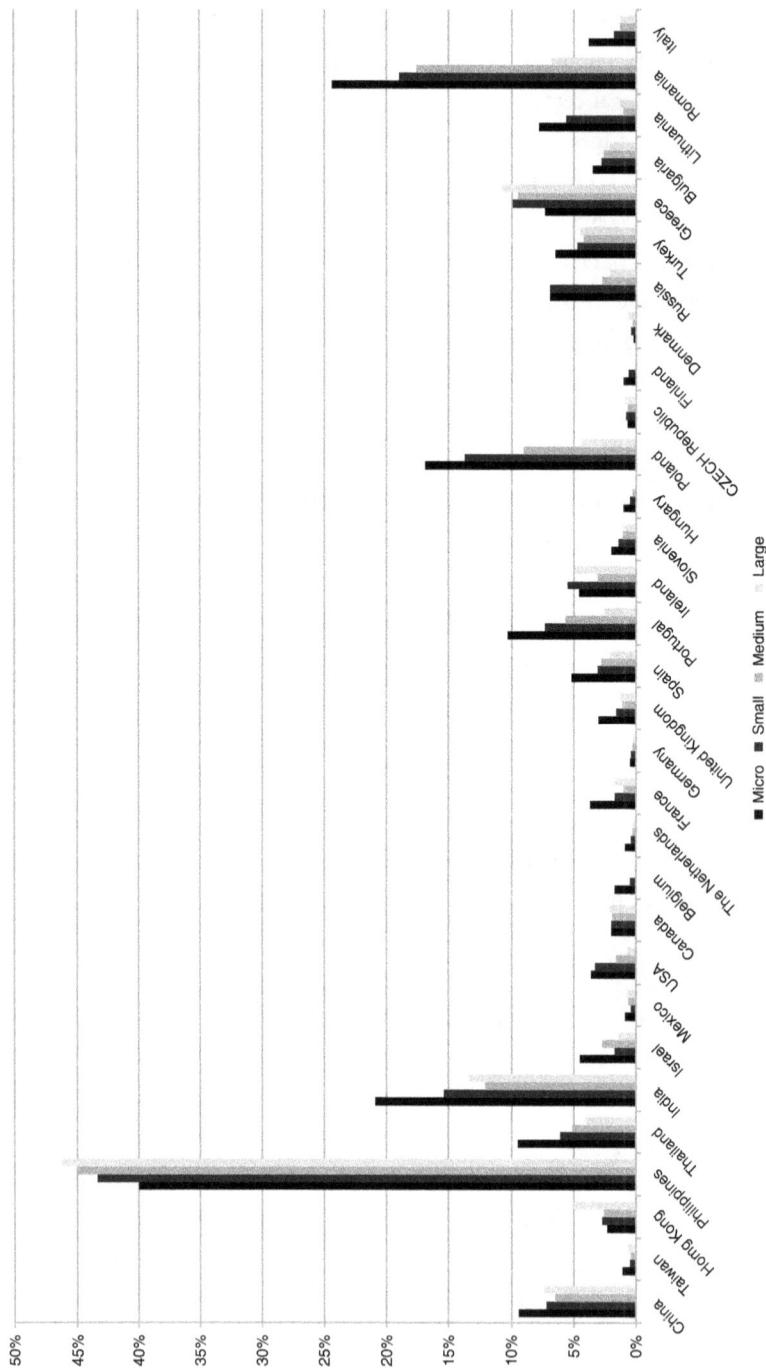

Figure 1.7 *Payments over 90 days by firm size*

Source: Author's elaborations of Cribis D&B data (2017).

Legend: ■ Micro ■ Small ■ Medium ▨ Large

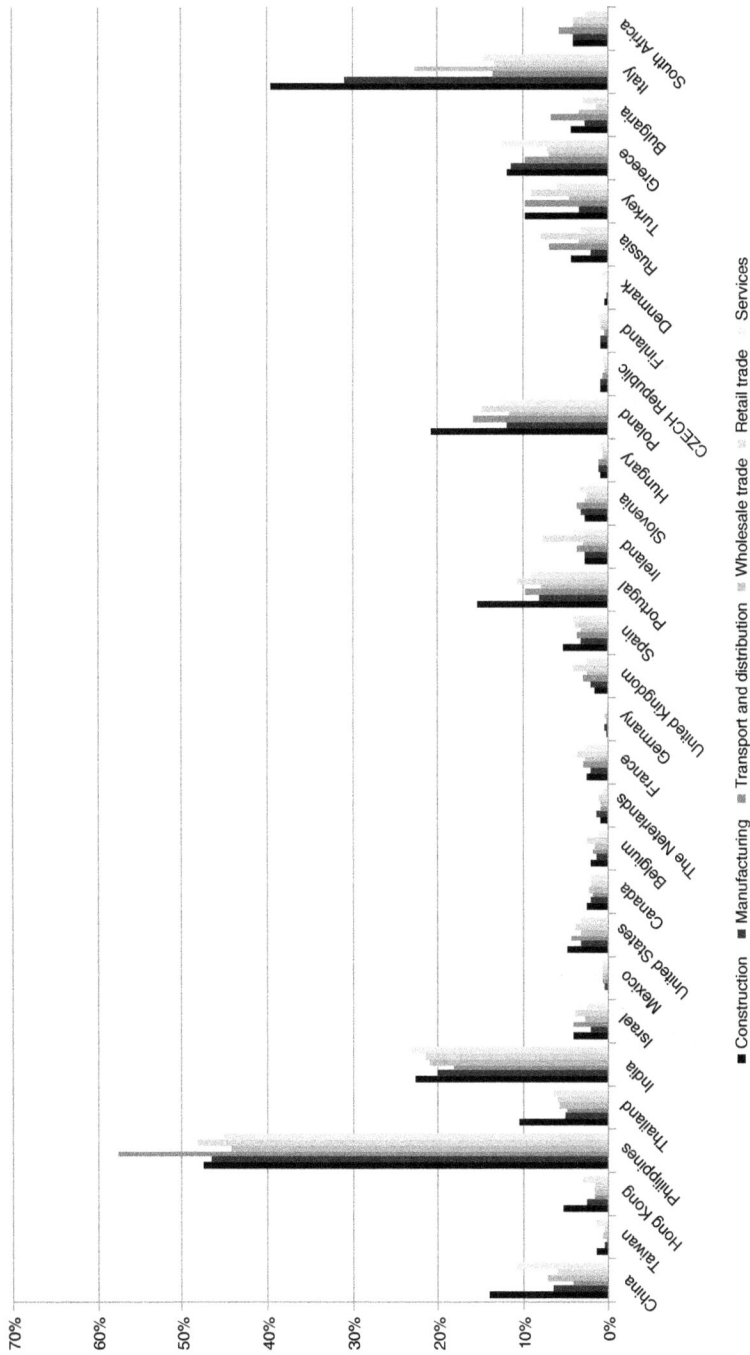

Figure 1.8 Payment practices over 90 days, by sector

Legend: Construction ■ Manufacturing ■ Transport and distribution ■ Wholesale trade ■ Retail trade ■ Services

Source: Author's elaborations of Cribis D&B data (2017).

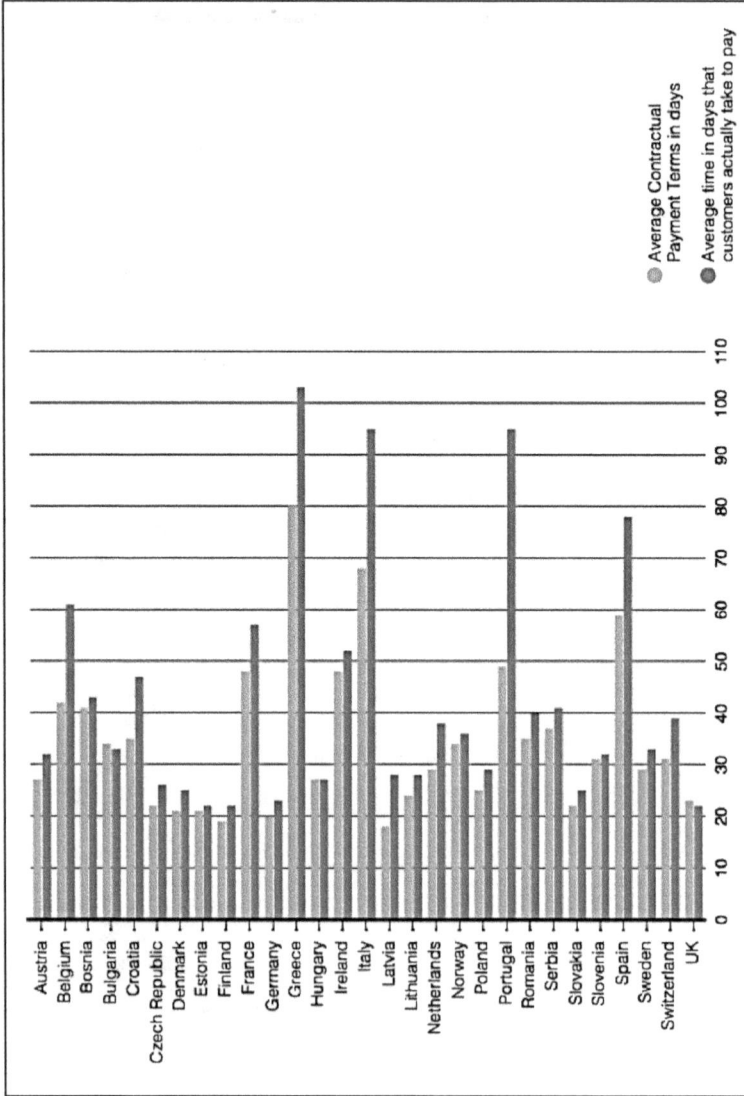

Figure 1.9 Payment practices in the public sector

Source: Intrum Justitia (2017).

lead to *PD* estimation that is not comparable in terms of underlying credit risk. Moreover, a nonmarginal incidence of counterparties is at risk of being classified as defaulted, even though they operate in sectors/geographical areas with a long payment duration. Because financiers are exposed to the credit risk of different counterparties originating from different commercial transactions, a more robust definition should be linked more to the impossibility of the counterparty paying any exposure over a given time horizon than to the breaching of a common threshold, because terms and conditions contribute to trade debt differentiation and the additivity of the past dues to verify the reaching of the critical value should be limited. Empirical evidence sheds light on the fit of the default definition to the trade credit financing activity. Table 1.4 shows the outstanding amount of nonperforming exposures for each quarter, based on the definition of *unlikely to pay* for financial intermediaries affiliated with the Italian Factoring Association (Assifact) with respect to domestic debtors, with the exclusion of public administration entities. Given the equivalent definition under the Basel II Capital Accord (column (a)), the table shows the results of investigating the contemporary past due classification (columns (b) to (g)), where the following thresholds are considered:

- Persistence of the past due exposure over 90 and 180 days.
- The amount of past due exposure over 1,000 euros and comprising more than 5 percent of the total amount of outstanding purchased/assigned trade credits.

Over the surveyed period, exposure to domestic debtors unlikely to pay shows that past dues of more than 90 days turn into higher-risk loans to a small extent and the introduction of other persistence and amount thresholds decreases the gap, with a smaller gap observed for the definition of default based on the absence of payment over 90 days. Such evidence confirms that, in trade credit financing exposures, distress is associated more with the trade debtor's inability to pay any credit over a prolonged period than with marginal unpaid exposure.

Table 1.4 Unlikely to pay exposures and default thresholds in trade credit financing exposures

Quarter	Unlikely to pay exposures (a)	Past due more than 90 days (b)	Past due more than 180 days (c)	Past due more than 1,000 euros (d)	Past due more than 180 days/ outstanding trade credits more than 5% (e)	Past due more than 180 days/ outstanding trade credits more than 5% persistent for 90 days (f)	Without any payment in 90 days (g)
December 2003	105,869,663	812,347,702	584,842,551	550,302,590	180,274,669	151,635,275	107,163,482
March 2004	111,268,056	666,853,378	386,574,767	357,124,981	187,988,943	154,885,376	112,958,166
June 2004	115,951,008	576,360,027	294,449,423	271,715,785	168,024,833	144,610,540	117,995,392
September 2004	115,516,306	719,606,664	304,493,107	280,337,509	152,572,586	140,188,451	117,548,138
December 2004	113,802,331	766,743,043	331,552,214	312,569,622	152,195,169	134,549,706	116,074,304
March 2005	117,056,887	622,509,164	345,453,657	307,749,310	160,177,430	147,472,520	118,525,978

Source: Author's elaboration of Assifact data

Once the default definition is set, the rating quantification requires the selection of one or more approaches to quantify risk. Each rating should map to a master scale showing the associated default probability (Bessis 2015). The broad alternative methods are (Altman and Saunders 1998)

- Equity-based methods, mainly for the rating quantification of listed counterparties
- Actuarial-based methods, developed based on historical defaults associated with each rating grade

Because the population of counterparties involved in trade credit financing comprises a high percentage of unlisted entities, the rating quantification is developed using mainly actuarial-based method. Given such a rating quantification, the following alternatives can be adopted (Carey and Hrycay 2001): a direct actuarial approach, a scoring approach, and mapping to rating agencies' grades. Regardless of the approach, the rating quantification for each grade must reflect a long-run average of the 1-year default rate for counterparties not belonging to the retail portfolio, as stated in the following equation:

$$\sum_{k=1}^{n} \frac{Def_k}{TDef} \times PD_{ik} \qquad (1.1)$$

where for $k=1,\ldots n$
    PD_{ik} is the PD estimated for grade i in year k
    Def_k is the number of defaults in year k
    $TDef$ is the total number of defaults over n years

Rating quantification measures are affected by the selected default definition. Figure 1.10 shows that, for UK companies accessing crowdfunding services, the annual default rate, based on the relation between the number of exposures in arrears and the total number of exposures, is under 10 percent and decreases over time. Application of equation (1.1) over 7 years to the entire portfolio of exposures results in a default

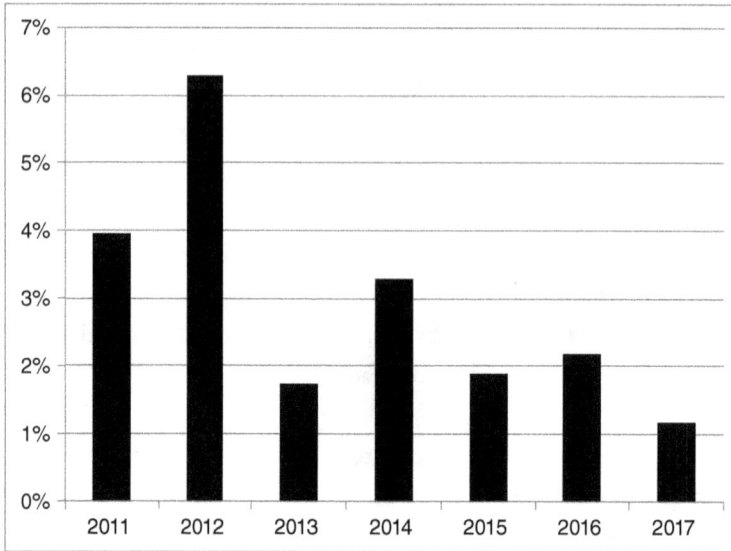

Figure 1.10 Default rate of trade credit financing exposures

Source: Author's elaboration of MarketInvoice data.

weighted mortality rate of 8.08 percent.[3] This evidence shows that strict past due definitions are consistent with average payment terms in that geographical area.

To ensure capital allocation consistency due to the slow payment habits characterizing some sectors and regions, such as the Euro-Mediterranean countries, default rates must be modified to favor an appropriate interpretation of technical defaults, that is, exposures that, after being classified in default because of qualified past dues, reenter performing status and/or are terminated without any loss. Empirical evidence shows that cash flow performance and residual credit capacity are not predictors of distress but can accelerate or delay distress in the presence of structural factors (De Leonardis and Rocci 2014). A common operative solution

---

[3]Even though the adopted default definition is not based on a minimum number of past due days, empirical evidence shows that more than 90 percent of such exposures are classified as crystallized losses. This category encompasses cases in which neither the seller nor the debtor repays the entire advance value plus interest. Therefore, these crystallized losses can be considered past due more than 90 days and used to forecast default risk (Dorfleitner, Rad, and Weber 2017).

adopted by financiers to reduce classification error is the modification of estimated *PD* values for each rating grade through the introduction of cure rates calculated according to the following equation:

$$\text{Cure rate} = \frac{N_{\text{cured}}}{N_{\text{default}}} \qquad (1.2)$$

where

N_{cured} is the number of defaulted exposures cured in period $t_0 - t_1$
N_{default} is the number of defaulted exposures in t_0

Starting with equation (1.2), it is possible to calculate cure rates for different periods and distress classifications and to assess the evolution along the years of the return in bonis of the exposures through marginal rates. Because whether and when the counterparty will return to the performing status are unknown, the survival analysis approach has found extended application in this context for the estimation of rates (Tong, Mues, and Thomas 2012). Available empirical evidence at the financial system level shows the following for corporate entities:

- Cure rates are volatile among financial intermediaries and migration among credit risk classifications stabilizes after 6 months (Piersante 2012). Such evidence is coherent with the European Banking Authority guidelines (2016) on the application of the default definition requiring a 3-month probation period.
- The ability of past due exposures to return to the performing status is correlated with GDP trends and sectors that affect cure rates (Boccuzzi 2015).
- The type of counterparty affects the ability of the distressed exposure to migrate to a riskier classification (Bonini and Caivano 2013).

Cure rates are very important for the estimation of *LGD* (see Loss Given Default section). The stronger the ability of exposures to be cured, the lower the expected *LGD*, with possible distortions of the reliability of credit risk factors (Hlawatsch and Ostrowski 2011).

Loss Given Default

Once default occurs, the trade credit financier must evaluate the loss that can manifest. *LGD* contributes to the facility rating via the amount of the exposure that will be lost by the creditor, because the study of debt recovery processes, even in more developed financial markets, usually highlights a success rate below the amount of initial exposure (Covitz and Han 2004).

After the manifestation of default, the financier's residual capital investment changes in terms of repayment sources, times, and costs (Gibilaro 2006a). The characteristics capable of affecting *LGD* can be either specific with respect to the characteristics of the individual credit exposures or general (Resti and Sironi 2007a). The former primarily comprise specific factors such as the following (Grunert and Weber 2009):

- Borrower characteristics. The literature on the influence of a company's legal form on debt recovery rates is limited at present. In the case of limited partnerships or listed companies, the lender is able to assert rights on the firm only through a judicial process. This specificity is important if the recovery rate of an individual exposure is assumed to be a function of the aggregate recovery rate of the company (Carey and Gordy 2004). Moreover, the higher the level of debt, the lower the expectation that the distressed firm's assets will be sufficient to satisfy all creditor categories. The recovery rates of subordinated exposures are lower than for the other exposures (Carty, Hamilton, and Moss 1999) and the gap increases with the debt cushion (Van de Castle and Keisman 2000) and the complexity of the financial structure (Hamilton and Carthy 1999), since debtors who have dynamically adjusted their capital structure are normally able to significantly reduce lender losses (Hackbarth, Miao, and Morellec 2006). Furthermore, larger companies could become marginally riskier—ex post—because financiers usually prefer not to immediately undertake recovery proceedings and tend to grant extensions and/or offer to renegotiate the loan (Asarnow and Edwards 1995). Apparently, however, these conclusions are not confirmed if one considers the amount of exposure instead of the size of the company, with respect to smaller enterprises as well (Davydenko and Franks 2008).

- Various aspects of the loan relationship. There is a negative relation between *LGD* and the degree of interrelation between bank and borrower and the length of their relationship. The greater the economic importance and the longer the relationship, the higher the likelihood that the borrower will honor its commitments, because otherwise other lenders on the market willing to offer credit under the same conditions would be very difficult to find (Berger and Udell 1995). The vintage is a proxy of the strength of the relationship between the customer and the financial intermediary. During the course of the relationship, the lender is able to collect more information about the customer (Longhofer and Santos 2003). This aspect is particularly important in the case of small firms, due to less information available, a shortcoming that can, however, be remedied by relationship lending in cases when the usual hard information is unavailable (Allen, DeLong, and Saunders 2004).

- Distinctive features of the financing contract. The facility features can contribute to mitigating the trade credit financier's risk. Guarantees requested by the lender could be classified as personal guarantees or collateral and the different types of guarantee offered could affect the usefulness in the recovery process (Peter 2006). In particular, while collateral reduces the expected *LGD* for any type of exposure, the current value of the personal guarantee does not affect the impact on the recovery rate. The collateral value could decline before the bank gains ownership of the asset and supervisors normally require the value of the covenant to be adjusted based on the expected value in the event of default (Frye 2000). The relevance of each type of guarantee for the *LGD* estimates depends on the law and the procedure established for the recovery process. The role of the guarantee also depends on its value with respect to *EAD*, with a higher ratio indicating a lower *LGD* for the contract analyzed. Due to economies of scale in the recovery process and its scheduling, efficacy is higher for larger exposures (Couwenberg and De Jong 2008). The great development of offensive mitigation techniques makes *LGD* sensitive to the usage of securitization, credit derivatives, and credit insurance contracts (Altman 2002). Beyond guarantees, the repayment schedule can also affect *LGD*. In revolving loans, borrowers are found to increase usage near default, with a positive impact on *LGD* (Zaniboni, De Araùjo, and De Avila Montini 2013). Lastly, disclosure of the transfer of the credit can be relevant. Nondisclosed assignments of credit can lead to mispayments by the trade debtor or losses due to the default of the seller/assignor in forwarding encashed credits (Gibilaro 2006a).

Systemic factors affecting *LGD* include macroeconomic variables approximating the economic cycle (Träuck, Harpainter, and Rachev 2005). The recovered amounts depend on the winding up of the defaulting borrower, on the sale of any guarantees or security provided, and on the enforcement of any bonds (Querci 2007). During periods of economic recession, increased insolvency above average long-term levels entails excess supply on the markets of assets disposed of by the banks to reduce the *LGD*. This causes prices to drop and reduces the overall value of the recoveries. Moreover, an excessive number of insolvencies could also affect the length of the recovery process, due to the increased activity of both the courts involved and the units responsible for the debt recovery operations (Giannotti and Gibilaro 2009).

Besides the economic cycle, several semispecific factors could affect recovery rates, depending on the composition of the lender's loan portfolio, such as the economic sector and the geographical area of operation. The borrower's economic sector could affect the characteristics of its balance sheet, determining a greater or lesser presence of intangible or tangible assets, different borrowing levels, and different degrees of asset liquidity (Izvorski 1997). The geographical location of the company's headquarters is important not only in the case of borrowers whose headquarters are outside the country and the company is therefore subject to different bankruptcy laws (Davydenko and Franks 2008) but also in the case of portfolios with a predominantly domestic component. Empirical evidence, in fact, has shown that, within a certain country, the competence of a particular court and/or location in a particular geographical area could determine different timeframes and/or success rates with respect to the recovery process (Bank of Italy 2001). This is also the case with respect to exposures with a low-risk profile, as in leasing transactions (De Laurentis and Riani 2005).

The influence of the specific and systemic variables discussed with respect to the recovery rates should ultimately be assessed in light of the operating and institutional characteristics of the creditor implementing the debt recovery process (Salas and Saurina 2002).

With regard to its operating characteristics, *LGD* is negatively related to the effectiveness and efficiency of the debt recovery process. The economic value of the recovery rates is negatively affected by the costs incurred by the financial intermediary and, through the discount rate applicable to the financial flows, the length of the recovery process (Gibilaro and Mattarocci 2007). Regarding the costs associated with the recovery activities, international empirical evidence shows that these differ according to the unit responsible. In particular, the direct internal costs incurred by specialized units are lower—by several percentage points—than those incurred by general units (Dermine and Neto de Carvalho 2006).

To quantify *LGD*, trade credit financier can measure the risk parameter through three approaches (Schuermann 2004):

- Market *LGD*, based on the observation of the market prices of defaulted bonds or marketable loans soon after the actual default event.
- Workout *LGD*, based on the estimation of cash flows resulting from the workout and/or collections process, properly discounted, and the estimated exposure.
- Implied market *LGD*. The estimation derives from risky but not defaulted bond prices or credit default swap spread using a theoretical asset pricing model to extract the risk premium and decomposing it into risk drivers. Compared with previous approaches, this allows one to consider that after-default scenarios can differ from bankruptcy and lead to cure, restructuring, and liquidation (Christian 2006).

Apart from the adopted approach, the risk parameter must reflect the economic loss and "when measuring economic loss, all relevant factors should be taken into account. This must include material discount effects and material direct and indirect costs associated with collecting on the exposure" (Basel Committee on Banking Supervision 2006, 102).

The application of the market and implied market *LGD* estimation approaches is suitable for the credit risk faced by investors with trade credit market instruments such as commercial papers and securitizations of receivables, even though evidence is limited. In any case, available empirical analysis shows that, for traded loans backed by trade credits, *LGD* exceeds roughly 10 percent and shows the lowest percentage after cash and securities (Carty, Hamilton, and Moss 1999).

International analyses have highlighted the difficulties in estimating the market *LGD*, especially for financial intermediaries (e.g., those in Europe) who do not frequently make public offerings of defaulted mortgage-backed securities (Araten, Jacobs, and Varshney 2004). Moreover, if the financier's policy is to service the defaulted assets, as most trade credit financiers do in light of their expertise, *LGD* estimation needs to be based on discounted workout recoveries (Brady et al. 2006).

Of the market instruments, the workout *LGD* approach is applicable to estimating the *LGD* of trade credit financing exposures. In detail, the risk parameter can be estimated through the following equation for each exposure:

$$LGD = 1 - \frac{\sum_{t=1}^{n} \frac{RF_t}{(1+i)^t} - \sum_{t=1}^{n} \frac{EF_t}{(1+i)^t}}{EAD} \qquad (1.3)$$

where
  RF_t is the recovery flow at time t, where the sign can be either positive or negative
  EF_t is the expense flow at time t
  i is the discounted rate of financial flows
  EAD is exposure at default

Identification of the financial flows characterizing the recovery process of trade credit financing exposures requires the availability of quantitative and qualitative historical information concerning default exposures. Table 1.5 shows the determinants of *RF*, *EF*, and *EAD* for each exposure. Because of potential bankruptcy clawbacks that can arise during the recovery process, *RF* can also take on a negative sign. Moreover, expense flow and recovery costs can be both specific and aggregate (i.e., the salaries of an internal legal department, the premiums for portfolio credit insurance). In particular, the latter require the proper approach to attribute them to single exposures through an analytic accounting system (ABI, 2002). The risk parameter *EAD* depends on the accounting value resulting from the balance sheet (Directive 2006/49/EC): Payments from trade debtors are classified among *RFs* when *EAD* coincides with the exposure determined by the advance to the seller/assignor.

Table 1.5 Workout LGD determinants

RF	EF	EAD
• Voluntary payments • Guarantees executions • Collateral executions • Credit insurance compensation • Settlement agreement • Bankruptcy clawbacks	• External legal assistance costs • Collection costs • Insurance premium	• Outstanding amount of trade credits • Advanced amount of trade credits

Source: Author's elaboration.

Calculation of the workout *LGD* requires financial flows to be properly discounted. In particular, financial flows must be discounted according to a rate consistent with an investment that possesses the following qualities (Basel Committee on Banking Supervision 2005a):

- Its amount equals the EAD.
- The time horizon is equal to the time interval between classification of the counterparty in default and the end of the recovery process.
- If relevant, nondiversifiable risk must be suitably covered in the spread relative to the risk-free rate.

The rates proposed in the literature for the selection of the discount rate are as follows (Gibilaro and Mattarocci 2007):

- The contract rate applied to the customer. The contractual loan rate approach requires that the flows recovered by the intermediary, after the state of insolvency is discovered, be discounted at the contract rate defined at the start of the relationship or at the last contractual rate renegotiated with the customer. This approach is deemed reasonable only if it is believed that the opportunity cost of the missing recovery of the sums upon the contract due date is correctly identified by this rate. This approach assumes that the insolvency event does not modify the risk of the operation.
- The risk-free rate. The decision to estimate LGD with the risk-free rate approach can result in underestimation because the current value of the flows generated by the recovery process would be computed without considering the greater degree of uncertainty that characterizes recovery flows.
- The risk-adjusted rate, estimated using a single-factor approach. This solution envisages the use of a discount rate corrected for the estimated risk by using a model with a similar formulation as the classical capital asset pricing model. This approach assumes the possibility of identifying an index representative of the market risk for all debtors considered in the estimation of LGD.
- The risk-adjusted rate, estimated using a multifactor approach. This approach extends the previous one by correcting the discount rate with multiple sources of variability during the recovery process, such as the debtor's industrial sector, the competent court for the recovery process, and the type of recovery process launched.

U.S. empirical evidence shows that trade receivables have a strong mitigating effect and the lowest levels of LGD, leading to a median percentage not exceeding 20 percent (Qi and Zhao 2011). Regarding European empirical evidence, trade credits are found to be highly significant and relevant in supporting recovery rates in France (Davydenko and Franks 2008). Empirical evidence on Italian trade credit financing exposures shows that, regardless of the type of discount rate applied, the average *LGD* is lower than 50 percent (Gibilaro and Mattarocci 2012). Moreover, evidence on the recovery process is sensitive to the selection of the discount rate, showing that the adoption of the contractual rate and the single-factor risk-adjusted rate determines higher *LGD* values, even though higher degrees of asymmetry and skewness are depicted. Moreover, the percentile distribution of the *LGDs* computed using different discount rates is not strictly comparable due to the significant differences in the value assigned to each percentile from the 30th to the 60th (Gibilaro and Mattarocci 2011).

Figures 1.11 and 1.12 illustrate updated insight on *LGD* not affected by choices of the discount rate from the crowdfunding experience. Based on crystallized losses, the *LGD* is determined as the ratio of the outstanding amount to the advance (Dorfleitner, Rad, and Weber 2017) and, because the average duration of the recovery process is shorter than 1 year (Figure 1.11), the discounting impact can be omitted, increasing the relevance of the effectiveness and efficiency of the recovery process. Although the average *LGD* from 2011 to 2017 is roughly 16 percent (Figure 1.12), modest variability is apparent in different years, showing a yearly range between 8.99 and 24.90 percent. Moreover, the median *LGD* is 0 percent in all the years considered. Therefore, the data show the positive skewness of the distribution, indicating that the vast majority of distressed

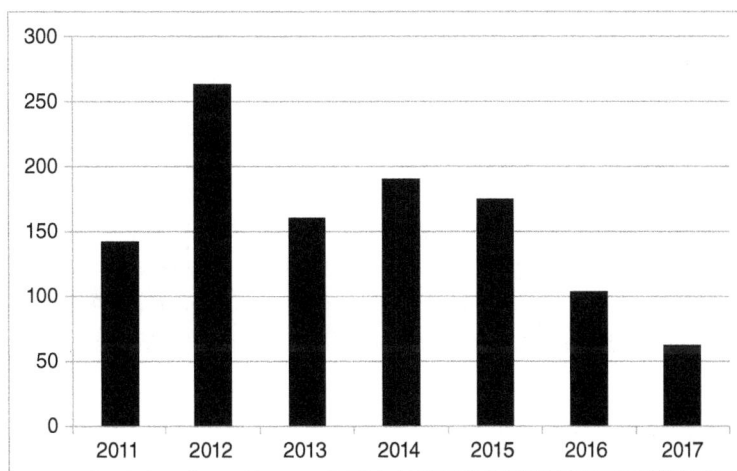

Figure 1.11 Duration of the recovery process of trade credit financing exposures days

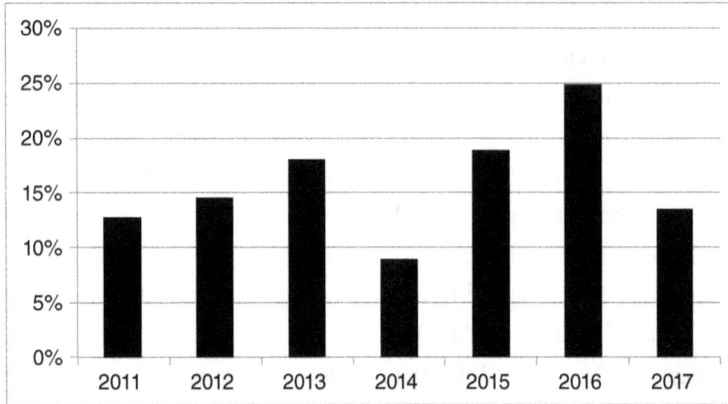

Figure 1.12 *LGD of trade credit financing exposures*

Source: Author's elaboration of data from MarketInvoice.

exposures terminate with an irrelevant loss. This finding is broadly consistent with the risk mitigation role played by trade credits, as well as in financial relationships where the financier is not privileged. The low loss rate can be attributed to the presence of a pair of counterparties for the recovery of the exposure due to the recourse nature of the transaction.

Empirical evidence also shows the relevant impact determined by the characteristics of the financing contract in trade credit financing exposures, such as transactional/relationship financing with the financier, the type of trade credits, and disclosure of the transaction to the financier (ABI 2002). In particular, by focusing on trade credit financing products offered by MarketInvoice,[4] it is possible to underline that future credits deriving from financing purchase orders and license fees determine the higher average *LGD*, signaling the highly unpredictable nature of future cash flows, while the financing of trade credits originated in the context of supply chains or regarding the whole ledger is associated with modest credit losses (Figure 1.13). Such results support the hypothesis in favor of enlargement of the business relationship information set to improve the prediction of credit risk.

---

[4]MarketInvoice's trade types are classified as follows: standard, whole ledger, purchase order, supply chain, license fee, multidebtor, and whole ledger. For a more detailed description of the products, see https://www.marketinvoice.com/solutions (last accessed 1/10/2018).

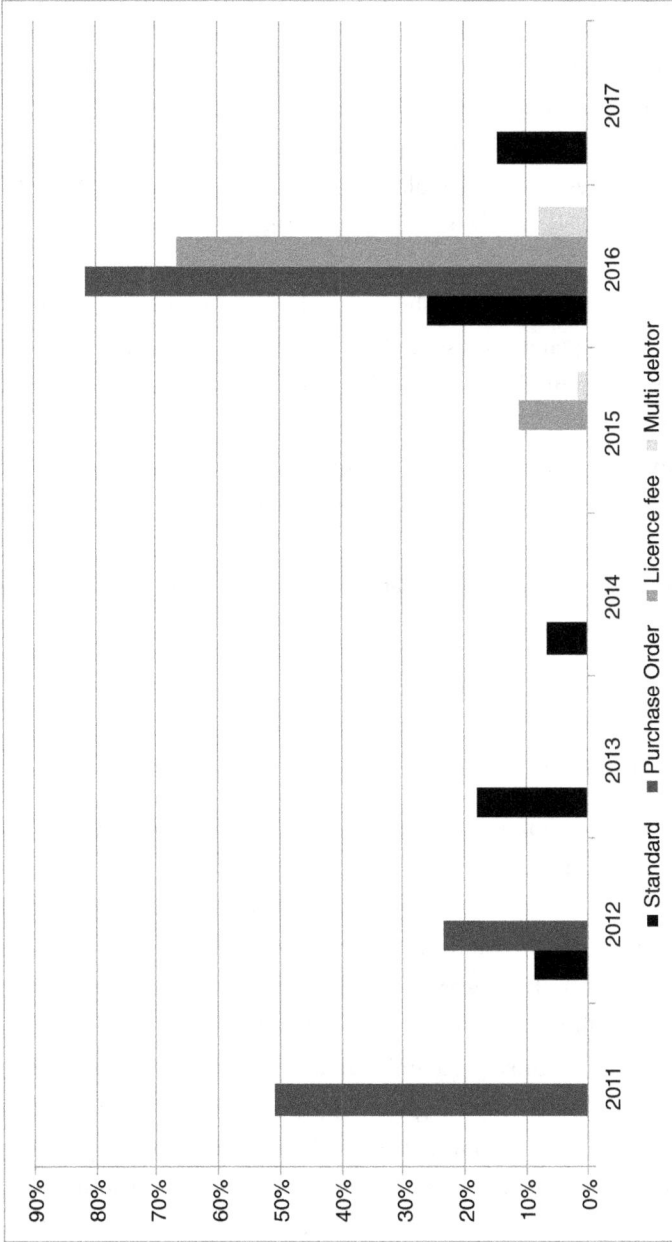

Figure 1.13 **LGD** *of trade credit financing exposures by product*

Source: Data from MarketInvoice, processed by the author.

LGD measurement methodologies span deterministic and stochastic approaches. Despite its significance, lookup tables are commonly used to calculate long-run average or median values of *LGD* for each bidimensional cell formed on the selected determinants, frequently reflecting the opinion of experts of what the *LGD* ought to be (Gupton 2005). Because of the asymmetric distribution of *LGD*, stochastic models are introduced and they refer to the following approaches (Qi and Zhao 2011; Hartmann-Wendels, Miller, and Toews 2014):

- Parametric approaches. The analyzed solutions refer to, like ordinary least squares regressions, fractional response regressions; inverse Gaussian transformation; and inverse Gaussian regression with a beta transformation.
- Nonparametric approaches. Frequently implemented methodologies refer to regression trees and natural networks.

Apart from the modeling methods adopted, trade receivables are found to deploy the strongest mitigating recovery rates (Qi and Zhao 2011).

Exposure at Default

The second dimension of the facility rating is the *EAD* and it determines the bank's potential loss when the debtor enters default status. The assignment of the facility rating based on *EAD* depends on the characteristics of both the debtor and the facility (Basel Committee on Banking Supervision 2004). The lower the credit rating, the greater the usage of residual credit lines (Asarnow and Marker 1995), even though better-rated firms tend to convert commitments in cash exposures to a greater extent, showing, on average, higher loan equivalents (Araten and Jacobs 2001). Credit risk mitigation through collateral determines higher loan equivalents (Jimenez, Lopez, and Saurina 2009) and the exposure is affected by the collateral type for nondefaulters (Zhao, Dwyer, and Zhang 2014). Since commitments purchased by firms show different levels of complexity (Schockley and Thakor 1997), *EAD* differs across different types of products (Araten and Jacobs 2001), and the predictability of the risk parameter is strictly affected by the relevance of the undrawn amount of the commitment (Asarnow and Marker 1995). Focusing on trade credit financing exposures, it is necessary to calibrate the determinants that the literature has identified as relevant in predicting *EAD*, as follows:

- Undrawn amount of the commitment. Trade credit financiers originate credit exposure by anticipating and/or guaranteeing trade credits. Therefore, they do not extend credit lines in favor of trade debtors that can be drawn discretionally. Trade credit financiers can contractually commit to buy trade credits in the future from the sellers/assignors, but this is frequently conditioned on both the enforceability and the amount. Therefore, *EAD* should distinguish between revocable/irrevocable and conditioned/unconditioned purchased trade credit commitments.
- Economic cycle phase. In light of the motivations determining the usage of trade credit with respect to the credit cycle (Meltzer 1960), *EAD* is expected to be strongly correlated with it.
- Alternative financing solutions. In light of the substitution relation between trade credit and financial credit (Lewellen et al. 1980), *EAD* can be affected by the possibility of customers paying suppliers by accessing other short-term financing instruments.

The rating quantification of *EAD* is based on the definition of the parameter in the Basel Capital Accords, which, for consistency, is set equal to no less than the current drawn amount, subject to recognition of the netting effect (Basel Committee on Banking Supervision 2006). Therefore, the variable component of *EAD* for each exposure is represented by the undrawn amount:

$$EAD = DA + CCF \times UA \qquad (1.4)$$

where
    DA is the current drawn amount
    UA is the current undrawn amount
    CCF is the expected credit conversion factor of the undrawn amount

In light of the recourse and nonrecourse assignment of receivables in trade credit financing, equation (1.4) yields different specifications. In particular, if the assignment of trade credits is with recourse to the seller/assignor, *EAD* can be determined as

$$EAD = A + CCF \times PA \qquad (1.5)$$

where

A is the current advanced amount
PA is the purchase agreement the financier has agreed upon with the seller/assignor
CCF is the expected credit conversion factor of the purchase agreement into the advanced amount

For trade credit financing exposures based on the assignment/sale of trade credits without recourse to the seller/assignor, the *EAD* can be determined as follows:

$$EAD = OUT + CCF \times PA \qquad (1.6)$$

where

OUT is the current outstanding amount of purchased/assigned trade credit receivables
PA is the purchase agreement that the financier has agreed upon with the seller/assignor
CCF is the expected credit conversion factor of the purchase agreement into the advanced amount

In both equations (1.5) and (1.6), prediction of *EAD* depends on *CCF*. Because of the clauses regulating the trade credit financier's commitment to purchase, the level of *CCF* will depend on the following:

- The revocable/irrevocable nature of the commitment. In particular, for revocable agreements, the seller's discretionary usage will decrease *CCF* when the trade credit financier can revoke the agreement without prior notification to the seller.

- The conditional/unconditional nature of the commitment. The commitment to purchase trade credits can be conditioned (i.e., absence of the deterioration of the credit risk of either the seller or the debtors), affecting both the enforceability and the amount of the agreed terms. Therefore, *CCF* will be lower.

Available empirical evidence shows that working capital financing is characterized by lower loan equivalents for nondefaulting counterparties, while it reaches the maximum, more than half the undrawn limit, when defaulted counterparties are considered (Zhao, Dwyer, and Zhang 2014). This finding can be interpreted in light of distress involving both trade debtors unable to repay their debt and a seller/assignor no longer able to sell/assign eligible trade receivables.

Maturity

Until now, it has been assumed that the duration of the exposure is irrelevant to the losses that the trade credit financier will realize when the counterparty enters default status. Nonetheless, increased risk is associated with longer-term facilities and lower risk is associated with very short-term facilities (Kirschermann and Norden 2012). Therefore, rating systems must factor in maturity to produce reliable capital allocation measures (Crouhy, Galai, and Mark 2001). *M* can be measured according to the following equation:

$$M = \sum_{t=1}^{n} t \times \frac{CF_t}{\sum_{t=1}^{n} CF_t} \qquad (1.7)$$

where
  t is the due date of the payment
  CF_t is the cash flow expected from the payment on the due date under contractual terms

Since trade credit financing exposures are involved, the prediction of equation (1.7) is based on the different types of due dates, depending on the contractual terms agreed with the seller and/or debtor when the trade credits are assigned/sold. The specific negotiated terms define the risk exposure horizon for the trade credit financier. In particular, depending on the product, it is possible to distinguish among the following exposure types:

- Nonrecourse exposure, both with and without advanced amounts
- Recourse exposure with advanced amounts
- Recourse exposures originating from anticipation of the value of future credits from contracts, licenses, and retainers

Under nonrecourse exposures, both with and without advanced amounts, the trade credit financier's risk exposure horizon is from the issuing date of the invoice to the encashment date of the trade credit. For recourse exposures with advanced amounts, the risk exposure of the trade credit financier is from the date of the advance of trade credits to their encashment date. Lastly, for exposures that originated from the anticipation of the value of future credits, the duration of the risk exposure can be determined as from the date of the advance of future cash flows to the expiration date of the limit agreed with the seller/assignor.

Since the previous specification of the risk exposure time horizon is involved, it must be pointed out that, at the moment of the sale/assignment of the trade credits to the financier, the due dates can be renegotiated with the seller. Such renegotiation introduces terms for the definition of the economic conditions for the supply of the services and, for example, the new due date can coincide with the duration of the assigned pool of trade credits, without notification to the trade debtor. Put differently, the trade credit financier can delay the due date of the payment through a new financing transaction agreed upon with the trade debtor, which will impact the encashment date.

Because of the stochastic nature of future cash flows, which, in the case of trade credit financing, can be determined by both liquidity and dilution issues, the forecast of M can be developed through estimation of the following parameters:

- Days of outstanding payments (DOP), that is, the time between the invoice assignment/sale date and the date of the payment encashment

- Days to credit maturity (*DCM*), that is, the time between the invoice assignment/sale date and the payment due date
- Days of outstanding payments from the advance (*DOPA*), that is, the time between the date of the advance of the invoice and the date of the payment encashment
- Days of payments from the credit maturity (*DPM*), that is, the time between the payment due date and the encashment date
- Days to credit limit maturity (*DLM*), that is, the time between the date of the extension of the advance of trade credits and the expiration date of the agreed limit with the seller/assignor.

Since the estimation techniques of *DOP*, *DCM*, *DOPA*, *DPM*, and *DLM* are involved, the solutions belong to long-run averages/medians but multivariate models can be developed given data availability. Figures 1.14 to 1.16 show, respectively, the trends of *DOPA*, *DCM*, and *DPM*[5] for trade credit financing exposures to corporate debtors originated through crowdfunding. Even though *DOPA* show a remarkable decreasing trend

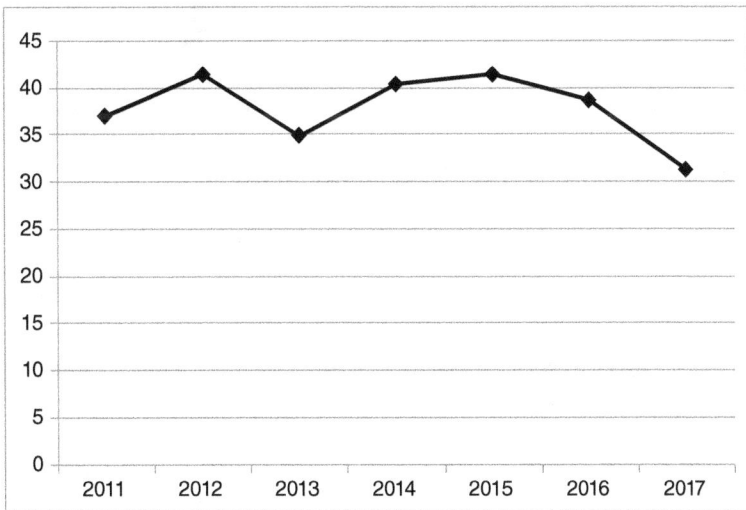

Figure 1.14 DOPA *trend (days)*

---

[5]Because MarketInvoice data consider only recourse financing, *DOP* and *DLM* are not implemented. The implementation of the measures excludes exposures for which the encashment depends on the recovery of losses.

over the last years, *DCM* are increasing, meaning that the average duration of the financier's risk exposure is increasing over time because of
either the extension of more generous payment terms by the trade creditor or the anticipation of the sale/assignment of the trade credits. Lastly,
DPM signal a large reduction in the average time to encash trade credits
with respect to the due date, which, in the last part of the observed time-
frame, even becomes negative, such that, on average, encashment antici-
pates the deadlines.

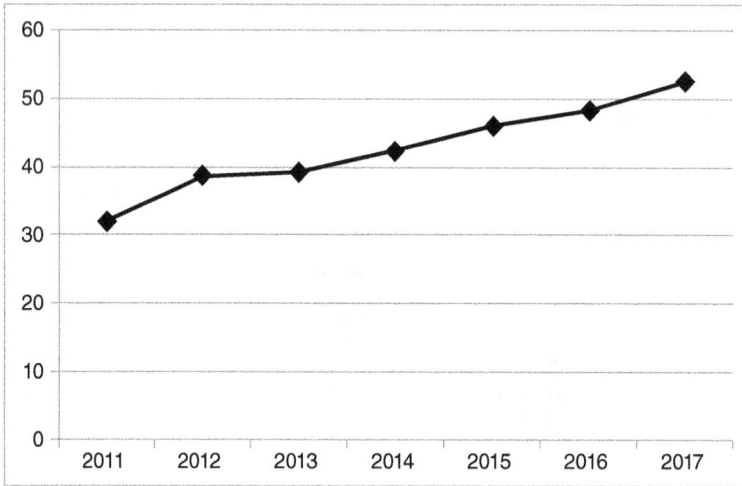

Figure 1.15 DCM *trend (days)*

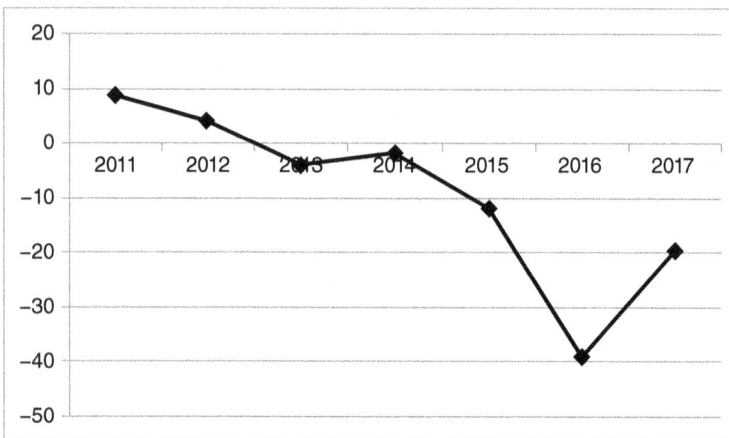

Figure 1.16 DPM *trend (days)*

Source: Data from MarketInvoice, processed by the author.

Dilution Risk

The relevant credit risk parameters in trade credit financing extend beyond the default of the counterparties to encompass dilution risk. As for other risk parameters, the risk source requires both assessment and quantification. The assessment of dilution risk[6] is based on the following determinants (Gibilaro 2006b):

- The type and the execution of the supply relationship. In particular, it is possible to distinguish between the supply of goods and services. Since this involves the supply relationship, the following aspects are important (Standard & Poor's 2004):
  - The vintage of the business relationship
  - The duration of the supply contract
  - The presence of performance clauses in the contract
  - The compensation rights
- The rating of the seller/assignor. It is expected that the lower the credit quality of the seller/assignor, the poorer the quality of the supply, implying a high chargeback rate (Dyckman 2011).
- The nature of the trade credits. In particular, future credits are exposed to events that can impact or meaningfully change the way typical deals will be executed in the future, with an expected positive impact on risk (Katz 2011).
- The disclosure of the sale/assignment of the trade credits. In particular, the undisclosed assignment of trade credits exposes the trade credit financier to commingling risk, that is, the possibility that direct payments will not reach the factor in the case of the seller's default between the notification of the obligors and the time they actually forward their payments to the factor (Association Française des Sociétes Financières 2003).

First, dilution risk is commonly quantified through an estimation of ELR_d at the supplier–customer level. The risk mitigation is very weak and, once the risk manifests, the amount of loss coincides with the exposure

---

[6]Hereinafter, ordinary dilution is considered.

due to the inefficacy of any recovery procedures. The parameter is defined as follows:

$$ELR_d = \frac{\text{Diluted Credits}}{\text{Outstanding}} \tag{1.8}$$

where

Diluted Credits is the amount of credits diluted during the time interval $t_0 - t_1$

Outstanding is the amount of credits at the end of period t_0

The relevance of dilution risk is marginal for trade credit financiers, such as factoring financial intermediaries. Table 1.6 reports the quarterly dilution loss rate of Italian factoring intermediaries affiliated with Assifact from 2003 to 2004. The data show a moderate impact of dilution risk, variable over time, and the tendency is confirmed at the geosectorial level. The same analysis reveals that ordinary dilution risk is associated with default risk, since more than half the population with dilution and default events overlaps.

Table 1.6 Quarterly dilution loss rate

March 2003	June 2003	September 2003	December 2003	March 2004	June 2004	September 2004	December 2004
1.47%	2.00%	0.98%	3.46%	1.33%	2.19%	1.71%	3.52%

Source: Author's elaboration of Assifact data.

In light of the relevance of the type of supply in determining the frequency of dilution risk, Table 1.7 shows the average quarterly dilution rate for each seller/assignor–trade debtor pair as classified by the economic sector branch[7] for Italian factoring companies. Although most of the pairs are characterized by an insignificant dilution rate, the following pairs of sectors are characterized by rates higher than 10 percent:

- Office machines, data processing machines, high precision, and optical instruments and paper, paper goods, newspapers, and publishing.

---

[7]Economic sectorial branches are defined according to: Bank of Italy (1991).

Table 1.7 *Average quarterly dilution loss rate % by sectorial branch*

Sectorial branch	051	052	053	054	055	056	057	058	059	060	061	062	063	064	065	066	067	068	069	070	071	072	073	Average
000	0	0	0	3	1	1	2	2	0	2	6	9	2	0	4	1	2	0	0	0	0	0	1	2
051	1	0	0	0	0	0	0	0	0	0	0	0	0	0	0	0	9	0	0	0	0	0	0	0
052	0	0	0	0	1	0	0	0	0	0	0	1	0	0	0	3	3	0	0	0	0	0	0	0
053	0	0	1	0	0	1	1	0	0	0	0	0	0	0	0	3	3	0	0	0	0	0	0	1
054	0	0	0	0	0	0	0	0	0	0	0	0	0	1	0	0	0	0	0	0	0	0	0	0
055	2	0	0	0	0	0	2	0	0	0	6	0	0	0	0	0	5	0	0	0	0	0	1	1
056	0	5	3	0	0	0	1	0	0	0	0	0	0	0	1	2	1	0	0	0	0	0	0	1
057	0	0	0	0	0	1	1	0	0	1	0	0	0	0	0	1	0	0	0	0	0	0	0	1
058	0	0	0	0	0	0	2	0	0	0	0	0	8	0	0	0	8	0	0	0	0	3	3	1
059	0	2	7	0	0	12	2	1	4	1	0	0	0	0	0	0	6	0	0	0	0	2	6	2
060	0	0	0	0	0	0	2	0	3	5	0	0	0	0	0	0	0	0	4	12	11	0	10	2
061	2	0	0	0	0	0	0	0	0	0	1	0	0	0	0	0	2	0	2	0	0	0	1	1
062	0	0	0	0	0	0	0	0	0	0	0	2	0	0	0	0	2	0	0	0	0	0	1	0
063	0	0	0	0	1	0	0	0	0	0	0	0	0	0	0	0	1	0	0	0	0	0	0	0
064	12	0	0	0	0	0	0	0	0	1	0	0	0	0	1	0	0	0	0	0	0	0	0	1
065	0	0	0	0	0	5	13	0	2	1	0	0	0	0	0	1	7	1	0	0	0	0	1	1
066	5	0	0	0	0	1	0	0	1	0	0	0	0	0	0	1	2	1	0	0	0	0	0	1
067	1	2	0	1	6	0	0	5	1	0	1	4	1	2	1	1	1	11	0	0	0	5	1	2
068	0	0	0	0	0	0	0	0	0	0	1	0	0	0	0	0	0	2	0	0	0	0	0	0
069	0	0	0	1	0	2	4	0	4	5	0	0	0	5	0	0	0	0	12	0	0	0	0	2
070	13	0	0	0	0	0	0	0	13	3	0	13	13	0	0	13	13	13	13	13	16	0	13	6
071	0	0	0	0	0	0	0	1	0	0	13	0	0	0	0	0	12	0	0	0	5	0	1	1
072	23	0	0	0	16	0	5	8	9	10	0	0	0	0	13	6	9	2	0	0	12	7	5	5
073	0	0	1	0	1	0	0	0	0	0	0	0	13	0	0	1	0	0	0	0	0	1	1	1
Average	2	0	1	0	1	1	1	1	1	1	1	1	1	0	1	1	4	1	1	1	2	1	2	

Source: Author's elaboration of Assifact data.

Note: For a full description of sectorial branch code, see the Annex.

- Office machines, data processing machines, and high precision and optical instruments and trade.
- Electrical material and supplies and minerals and ferrous and non-ferrous metals, excluding fissile and fertile metals.
- Transportation vehicles and maritime and air transportation services.
- Transportation vehicles and maritime and air transportation services and services to transportation.
- Rubber and plastic products and products of agriculture, forestry, and fishing.
- Other industrial products and agricultural and industrial machines.
- Transportation services and transportation services.
- Maritime and air transportation services and electrical materials and supplies/textile products, leather and footwear, and clothing/paper, paper goods, newspapers, and publishing/building and public works/trade/hotels and other public services/transportation services/maritime and air transportation services/services to transportation/other trade services.
- Communication services and products of agriculture, forestry, and fishing/chemical products/other industrial products.

Moreover, it is possible to observe high and persistent dilution rates for suppliers from the following sectors, regardless of the sector with which they are paired:

- Maritime and air transportation services
- Communication services

Analysis of the same data for the type of contract determining the trade credit financing exposure shows that non-notification contracts have the highest dilution rate, followed by contracts stating payments at maturity and the advance of subsidies extended by the public sector, while other types of contract have dilution rates of less than 2 percent (Table 1.8).

Table 1.8 Dilution rate by the type of the contract

Contract type	Average dilution rate (%)
Not disclosed assignments with advanced amounts	15.86
Recourse maturity assignments	6.01
Nonrecourse maturity assignments	5.65
Advance of subsidies extended by the public administration	5.53
Nonrecourse assignments with management of trade credits	4.14
Nonrecourse advance of trade credits	2.52

Source: Author's elaboration of Assifact data.

Loss rates determined by dilution risk are shown to be variable and, for some sectors and contractual types, insignificant. Because the dilution risk mitigation of loss rates is expected to be weak, careful analysis must focus on exposure to risk that differs from default risk. In the case of dilution risk, the following must be distinguished:

- Exposures in which the risk occurs during execution of the business relationship
- Exposures in which the risk occurs after execution of the business relationship

In relation to the former, exposure to ordinary dilution risk exists only in transactions that advance trade credits. The underlying commercial relationship can cause the outstanding to be offset only for the anticipated part exposed to potential disputes with the debtor (Figure 1.17). By broadening the definition to extraordinary events, in the absence of the financial component, *EAD* cannot be considered null. The risk of dilution can certainly occur after the termination of the supply and the maturity date of the credit (Figure 1.18). By comparing Figures 1.17 and 1.18, it appears that the exposure to risk is not strictly connected with the contractual terms of the sale/assignment of the trade credits but, rather, depends on the moment of the manifestation of dilution with respect to the financial outflow of the trade credit financier.

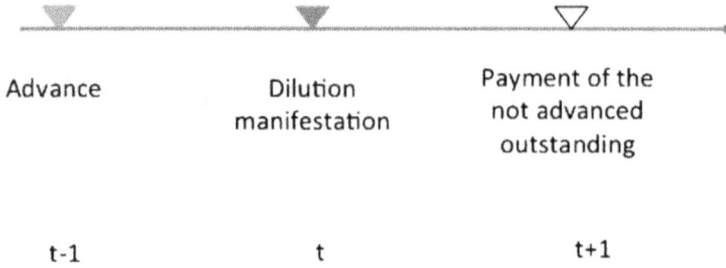

Figure 1.17 Exposure when dilution equals the advance

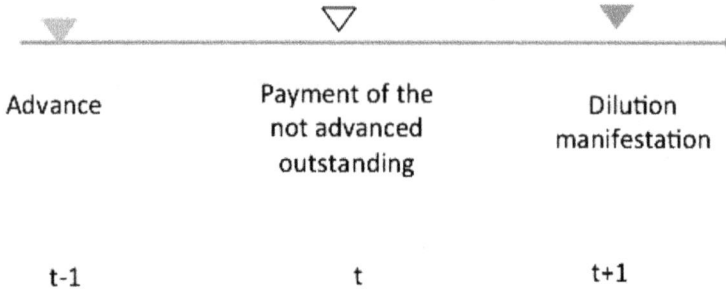

Figure 1.18 Exposure when dilution equals the outstanding

Source: Gibilaro (2006b).

Since the maturity of the exposure to dilution risk is involved, it must be underlined that this maturity is shorter for ordinary dilution and typically does not exceed a quarter, since disputes will be uncovered before the due date of the trade credit. Put differently, if extraordinary dilution is considered, the maturity is longer and matches the deadline of the payment, which is thus less than 1 year, in light of the typical duration of commercial payments.

Concentration Risk: Alternative Approaches and Empirical Evidence

Analysis of the relevance of single name and sectorial/geographic concentration requires the adoption of indicators that take into account the characteristics of financiers' portfolios.

The significance of the concentration risk estimated through the single name approach in financial and commercial operations can be analyzed by considering exposure to the major client counterparties with respect to the total credit portfolio. In particular, such a risk profile can be assessed by building a concentration relationship relative to the n major customers and comparing the results with respect to financial and commercial credit operations (Norden and Szerencses 2006). This can be written as

$$CR = \sum_{i=1}^{n} \frac{Exp_i}{Exp_{TOT}} \qquad (1.9)$$

where

Exp_i is the exposure to a major customer

Exp_{TOT} is the total exposure of the financier

In light of the available literature, the analysis of sectorial/geographic concentration risk uses indexes that are most extensively used to assess the degree of concentration/entropy of customer portfolios (Heitfield et al. 2005). More in detail, the following indexes can be considered:

- Gini index
- Entropy indexes

The measure proposed by Gini (1936) represents an estimate of the dispersion of observations with respect to a theoretical distribution that ensures a fair distribution of the credit portfolio. This can be stated as follows:

$$G = \frac{2}{n-1} \sum_{i=1}^{n} \left(Exp_i - \widehat{Exp_i} \right) \qquad (1.10)$$

where the concentration depends on the difference between the real distribution of n observations (Exp_i) with respect to the theoretical distribution that represents the equitable distribution of the assets (Exp_i). In the presence of distributions characterized by a limited number of observations and a non-negligible degree of asymmetry and/or kurtosis, the indications provided by such an index could prove misleading (Hart 1971).

The entropy indexes, on the other hand, are not based on a comparison with an optimum theoretical distribution, since they merely measure lack of homogeneity in the distribution, attributing different weights in relation to the extent of the deviations (Shannon 1948). The most widespread formulation provides for the calculation of a weighted average of the relative exposures:

$$H = \sum_{i=1}^{n} \frac{\dfrac{Exp_i}{Exp_{TOT}} \log\left(\dfrac{Exp_i}{Exp_{TOT}} \right)}{\log(n)} \tag{1.11}$$

where the value of the index increases as the concentration of the investments increases $\left(\dfrac{Exp_i}{Exp_{TOT}} \right)$ according to a weighting factor derived from the logarithmic function $\left(\log\left(\dfrac{Exp_i}{Exp_{TOT}} \right) \right)\left(\log\left(\dfrac{Exp_i}{Exp_{TOT}} \right) \right)$.

The available empirical evidence contributes to establishing a positive relation between concentration and risk only when sectorial/geographical concentration is considered. The average exposure concentration index for commercial credits is always higher than 50 percent. Analysis of the degree of entropy shows that concentration proves to be much more variable in nonrecourse transfers than in the other commercial operations (Table 1.9).

Table 1.9 *Concentration differences for commercial credits*

		Gini index			Entropy index		
		Mean (%)	Max (%)	Min (%)	Mean (%)	Max (%)	Min (%)
Commercial credits	Overall	53.22	59.04	46.98	68.36	69.09	67.10
	Recourse credits	53.64	57.87	47.70	72.89	73.82	72.15
	Nonrecourse credits	56.43	63.24	49.73	61.69	63.08	59.75

Source: Gibilaro and Mattarocci (2009).

By using the concentration measures, in just a few comparisons of the defaults and portfolio composition during the preceding quarter, one can see close correspondence between the more relevant regions/sectors and the characteristics of the counterparts that are the most affected by default. Different results are obtained if, instead of close correspondence, one considers a relation between an above-average (below-average) concentration and the presence (absence) of insolvency phenomena. Such a relation can be investigated by considering four subgroups for each quarter, that is, sectors/regions which, in the preceding quarter, witnessed concentration levels above the median value and sectors/regions that, during the quarter, reported a number of defaults above or below the median value. In most cases, the branches where the credit portfolio is more concentrated are also those that prove riskier ex post, while a prevailing association is noted when considering geographic profiles (Table 1.10).

Table 1.10 *A comparison between starting exposure and defaults*

	Coherence between starting exposure and defaults for each category*			Coherence between starting exposure and defaults for group of categories**		
	Median (%)	Max (%)	Min (%)	Median (%)	Max (%)	Min (%)
Sectoral classification	13.16	26.32	5.26	92.54	94.74	78.95
Geographical classification	9.1	21.05	0.00	50.00	63.16	36.84

*The coherence is studied comparing quarter-by-quarter regional and sectorial rankings for defaults at current quarter and starting exposure of previous quarter.
**The comparison for groups is released considering only two subgroups (best and worst) for defaults at current quarter and starting exposure of previous quarter.
Source: Gibilaro and Mattarocci (2009).

Conclusions

The application of standard credit risk measures to trade credit financing can produce consistent estimations of potential losses, even though the peculiarities of the business require the calibration in light of the more complex system of risk sources associated with credit losses.

An internal rating system was developed based on the acknowledgment of optionality in the recognition of trade credit among risk mitigation techniques, leaving room for both an asset and a relationship approach, depending on how the trade credit is managed by the financier. Moreover, the system addresses the dual nature of credit losses, that is, default and dilution driven.

In light of the importance of the counterparty in the total portfolio, the measurement of the *PD* follows both bottom-up and top-down approaches. To predict the *PD*, trade credit financiers use a diversified information data set, coherent with the broad range of types of counterparties among which a trade credit relationship can exist. The definition of default is a relevant issue in trade credit financing, particularly with prolonged average payment terms. Therefore, proper qualifiers of the relevance of the past dues with respect to total supply chain exposures should be introduced. Trade credits are found to improve the reliability of forecasts, and the shift from assets to supply chain relationships is associated with an improvement in recovery rates. Even though trade credit financiers' exposures are not characterized by optionality of usage for the seller/assignor, the terms of the trade credit purchasing program can increase risk, while recognition of the effective maturity can reduce risk because of the short-term encashment periods.

Exposure to dilution risk is determined by the discovery of the event with respect to the trade credit financier's financial performance. Even though, at the aggregate level, the risk is moderate, original empirical evidence shows that the impact of the risk is variable over time, connected with the types of economic sectors involved in the transactions and affected by the type of contract.

Given the concentration that structurally characterizes the trade credit exposure of financiers, the measures implemented are not associated with relevant credit losses or the single name or geographical/sectorial perspective, suggesting that the measures should address the excess concentration in the origination of additional losses.

CHAPTER 2

Application of Credit Risk Measures to Internal Processes

Introduction

Credit risk parameters are instrumental to the convergence of the capital financiers need to hold and the losses suffered by creating a risk-oriented organization, but the effectiveness of the reduction of the misalignment is strongly affected by the application to a broad range of internal processes, as required by the Basel Capital Accords to obtain regulatory capital relief.

First, credit risk parameters can be applied to originate new exposures apart from the considered portfolio (see Credit Risk Origination section). Then, to align ex ante and ex post risk exposure, the credit risk parameters are applied to define limits and monitoring and select the exposures to transfer (see Credit Risk Control section). Lastly, several applications of credit risk parameters are introduced in the auditing, reporting, management, and administration processes (see Credit Risk Management section). Concluding remarks are presented in Conclusions section.

Credit Risk Origination

The ex ante coherence between the trade credit financier's risk appetite and the underwritten risk is based on the application of credit risk parameters to the origination process of new exposures. Such an application can even represent a vehicle for maintaining lending standards (Treacey and Carey 2000). In particular, hard information lending techniques, such as credit scoring, give loan officers high-power incentives without compromising the integrity and quality of the loan approval process (Heider and Inderst

2012). Such an increase in performance, resulting in the better prediction of defaults, is particularly remarkable when associated with long-term relationships among the organizational units participating in the origination process (Qian, Strahan, and Yang 2015). Cross-border surveys on the applications of credit ratings state that most financial intermediaries link the credit authorization process to credit risk parameters (Basel Committee on Banking Supervision 2000), introducing a negative relation between loan approval decisions and risk grades (Agarwal and Wang 2009), separate from the selected segment (Crouhy, Galai, and Mark 2001). At the country level, available surveys show that the application of internal ratings in loan approvals has increased over time and their adoption by financial intermediaries has not been affected by the global financial crisis (Del Prete et al. 2014), even though the extension of financing to small- and medium-sized enterprises (SMEs) was moderated by the usage of credit scoring techniques (Del Prete et al. 2017). Figure 2.1 shows that the adoption of the internal ratings to authorize new corporate exposures is comparable to monitoring. Moreover, the larger the bank, the more relevant the usage of internal ratings, even though it has diminished over the years.

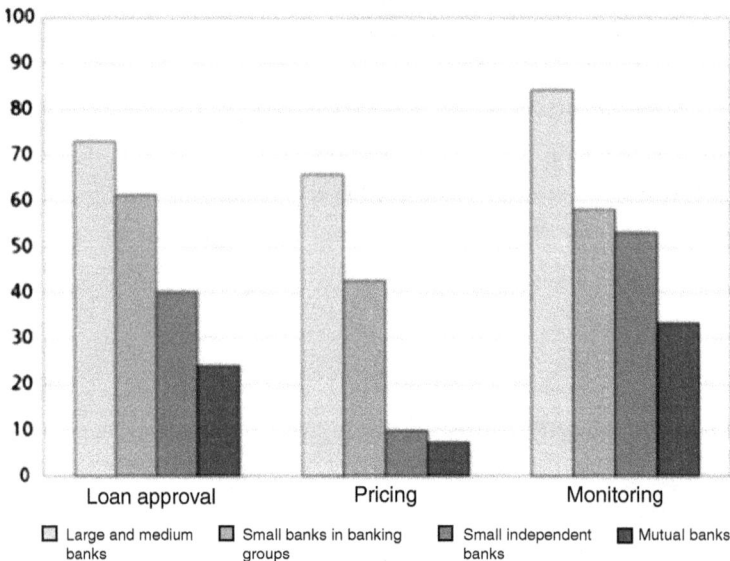

Figure 2.1 *Internal ratings and bank size*

Note: Frequencies are weighted by loans extended to firms by respondent banks.
Source: Del Prete et al. (2014).

A relevant issue in the application of internal ratings for new exposure origination is the high sensitivity to the business cycle when a point-in-time philosophy is adopted (De Laurentis, Maino, and Molteni 2010). This feature deserves further investigation by financial intermediaries for corporate and SME exposures, whereas for retail exposures, they strongly prefer a point-in-time philosophy (Associazione Italiana Financial Industry Risk Managers (AIFIRM), 2016).

Recent empirical evidence shows that, even though loan officers rely on hard information, as in the case of ratings, evaluations can still be manipulated (Berg, Puri, and Rocholl 2013).

Credit Risk Control

Once the financier has developed credit risk metrics for trade credit financing exposures, credit risk control is instrumental to ensure that risk is, ex ante, consistent with shareholders' preferences (Saita 1999). This goal is based on the following:

- Establishment of limits
- Monitoring and revision of credit risk ratings
- Deciding which risks to transfer and which to retain

In particular, the establishment of risk limits is based on the application of the credit risk metrics at different levels (Spuchľáková, Valaškováb, and Adamko 2015). For trade credit financiers, these limits are the following:

- Single counterparty, that is, either seller/assignor or trade debtor. Such a limit allows risk to be controlled by avoiding counterparties under a predefined PD threshold and limiting single name concentration.
- Seller/assignor–debtor pair. Such a limit is consistent with risk sources in trade credit financing and is based on the expected loss for default risk (EL) and dilution risk (EL_d) for the relationship.
- Sectorial/geographical areas. At this level, the limits are targeted at stemming excess concentration by sector/geographical area.

- Countries. This limit is a more aggregated level, but it allows risk to be controlled, particularly when financing cross-border supply chains.

Once the limits are set, coherence between the risk measures, limits, and effective risk must be ensured. Consequently, trade credit financiers must monitor the condition of individual credits, including the adequacy of provisions and reserves. Moreover, the monitoring must also cover the portfolio level (Basel Committee on Banking Supervision 2000).

Effective monitoring is targeted at

- Early and timely detection of an increase in credit risk
- Controlling risk by monitoring of EAD
- Effective measures to strengthen the recovery process

Particularly for trade credit financing, monitoring is found to obtain updated information from multiple commercial payments on the counterparty's creditworthiness that can be useful in promptly implementing actions (Mester, Nakamura, and Renault 2007). The phases of the monitoring can be outlined as follows:

- Detection of a decrease in the counterparty's creditworthiness
- Identification of the potential causes of the decrease in creditworthiness
- Definition of the management actions to take
- Management of the exposures on the watch list and classification of potential defaults

Concerning the first phase, detection is realized through ongoing control based on both expert judgment and automated scoring models. In light of the multiple commercial payments that can be observed for each trade debtor, the effectiveness of the controls depends on the reconciliation of payments, which is affected by the type of payment instrument and on the time required to allocate payments to trade debtors. The information from the ongoing control of the trade credit financier is summarized in Table 2.1. Potential monitoring indicators differ depending on the information source and area.

Table 2.1 Information from the ongoing control

Source	Area	Monitoring indicators
Exposure type	Assignments of trade credits with advance	• Drawn amount higher than the outstanding trade credits that can be financed (i.e., assigned trade credits net of past due trade credits from more than 60 days) by more than 20–40% • Drawn amount higher than the outstanding trade credits that can be financed (i.e., assigned trade credits net of past due trade credits from more than 60 days) higher by more than 20–40% of the assigned outstanding amount
	Assignments of nonrecourse trade credits without advance	• 60 days past due credits higher more than 30% of nonrecourse credits • Outstanding credits past due more than 90 days
Business relationship	Disputes among trade creditor and trade debtor	• Frequency • Relevance of relationships involved in the disputes for either the seller/debtor
Seller/assignor behavior	Reconciliation of payments	• Payments made directly to the seller • Interruption of new assignments • Missed or late forwarding of encashments by the seller/assignor

Source: Author's elaboration.

Once default has been detected, the financier must identify the potential causes of the decay in creditworthiness to evaluate the allocation to the watch list. In particular, the following aspects must be carefully considered:

- The ability of the observed event to be reconciled with the assigned rating class. In trade credit financing, it can be particularly important to obtain the reconciliation in light of the broad source of information affecting the rating attribution and the multiplicity of trade payments of each debtor.
- Managerial actions must be coherent with the rating class.
- The coherence between the qualitative elements of the rating attribution and the observed events. In particular, qualitative elements

should allow the rating attribution to be forward looking and able to obtain updates from the monitoring.

Exposures that are classified on the watch list, the third phase of the monitoring process, require a hypothesis concerning the future of the exposure, that is, to be reclassified as either a performing exposure or a gradual decline in creditworthiness. Regardless of the hypothesis, the trade credit financier is required to define the new contractual features in terms of prices, collaterals, and amount drawn.

Lastly, the trade credit financier must control the deliberated actions. In particular, because the trade credit financier frequently reschedules when the trade credits are assigned, possible impacts on past dues must be controlled in order to avoid artificially inflating the cure rate.

Outcomes from monitoring can determine rating revisions. In particular, for trade credit financing exposures that allow one to observe payment performance at a very low frequency due to the multiplicity of commercial payments to multiple creditors, the revisions can be timely, with a prompt cascade effect on contract terms, and, all else being equal, they should be less frequent under high-quality monitoring (Coleman, Esho, and Sharpe 2006).

Once the rating enters the revision phase, either because of events observed during monitoring or because ratings are planned on a regular basis, it is very important that the process not be affected by any conflict of interest among the counterparties to the decision (Mehran and Stulz 2007) potentially delaying rating modification (Barber, Lehavy, and Trueman 2007), that is, found to be less relevant when institutional investors own the rating entity (Ljungqvist et al. 2007). In particular, distortions are potentially affected by the following (Saita 2004):

- The type of segment considered. Ratings assigned through more automated approaches are expected to be less exposed to deliberately detrimental variations.
- The owners of the information instrumental to the revision. If the revision gathers copious amounts of information in managing the relationship with the customer, the opportunity to alter the rating is expected to be greater.

- The size of the entity. The party deliberating the alteration of the rating will have a stronger incentive the larger the entity.

The last instrument to control risk is the choice of risks to transfer. Because of the two potential sources of credit risk, the choice concerns the following:

- Default risk. Trade credit financiers are ordinarily actively involved in managing credit risk. Therefore, they transfer risks exceeding a previously fixed limit or a deductible can be established whereby the insured financier will assume this first level of loss for its own account (Jones 2007).
- Dilution risk. Depending on the firm-specific nature of the risk, trade credit financiers will not outsource it, preferring internal mitigation measures. In particular, such internal measures converge on (a) overcollateralization through the application of a haircut to the financed outstanding of account receivables with respect to the advanced amount (Katz 2011) and (b) process standards, such as greater transparency, fast response times, adequate control over buyers (Hofman and Belin 2001), and legal disclosure of the assignments of trade credits (Gibilaro 2006a).

Credit Risk Management

The measurement, origination, and control of credit risk are instrumental to risk management, pursuing the goal of efficiently allocating capital under a dynamic scenario in the face of exposure to unhedged risks (Froot and Stein 1998). When thinking about acceptable levels of volatility and the capital to support it, many financiers consider value at risk (*VaR*), that is, the amount of economic capital necessary to cover unexpected credit losses at a chosen confidence level (Nocco and Stulz 2006). In other words, the *VaR* corresponds to the difference between the chosen quantile of the distribution and the expected credit loss.[1]

---

[1]For a broader discussion of *VaR*, see Jorion (2007).

Table 2.2 *Expected loss rate (ELR), unexpected loss rate (ULR), and VaR in trade credit financing*

Default risk	Dilution risk
$ELR = PD \times LGD$	ELR_d
$ULR = \sigma(ELR)$	$ULR = \sigma(ELR_d)$
$VaR = L^{\text{confidence interval}} - ELR$	$VaR_d = L_d^{\text{confidence interval}} - ELR_d$

Source: Author's elaboration.

Credit risk capital allocation for trade credit financiers covers both default and dilution risk (Table 2.2). While expected loss (*EL*) can be decomposed into the *PD*, *LGD*, and *EAD*, EL_d is measured directly. In both default and dilution risk, the variability around *EL* that is affected by maturity determines the unexpected loss (UL).

Capital allocation against credit risk starting with *VaR* to determine the capital to absorb potential losses at a given confidence interval is called capital at risk (*CaR*). Use of *VaR* to allocate capital is based on a longer time horizon because it is connected with the time horizon for preserving the solvency of institutions (Resti and Sironi 2007b).

For trade credit financiers, *CaR* must reflect the twofold nature of the risk but it needs to consider that exposures hit by dilution risk cannot be hit by credit risk and vice versa. Therefore, *EAD* must be adjusted. Consequently, *CaR* can be calculated as

$$CaR = VaR_d \times EAD + VaR \times (EAD - VaR_d) \qquad (2.1)$$

The determination of *CaR* allows several applications of risk management to managerial processes. In particular, such applications concern the following (De Laurentis 2001):

- Process auditing
- Portfolio reporting
- Credit management
- Credit administration

Process auditing addresses the opportunity to review the effectiveness and efficiency of internal processes that are exposed to credit risk.

Table 2.3 Data pooling for validating dilution risk drivers

Category	Information	Type of the information
Supply relationship	Economic sector (SIC code) of seller and buyer	Objective
	Degree of replacement of the supply	Objective/subjective
	Commercial policy of the seller	Objective/subjective
	Market power of the seller	Objective/subjective
	Performance clauses	Objective
	Vintage of the supply relationship	Objective
	Transactional/occasional supply relationship	Objective/subjective
Type of trade credits	Existing trade credits	Objective
	Future trade credits	Objective
Legal structure of the sale/assignment of trade credits	Notification of the assignment	Objective
	Recognition of the assignment	Objective
	Other legal clauses	Objective

Source: Author's elaboration.

First, process auditing involves the internal rating process, with the aim of verifying ex post performance, that is, the ability of internal ratings to classify exposures correctly. In particular, this activity is based on the validation of both out-of-time and out-of-sample risk measures.[2] One issue with such an application is the availability of a broad historical database, which small trade credit financiers can overcome by merging external sectorial sources, as in data pooling. Table 2.3 reports information that can be shared through a data pooling initiative to validate dilution risk drivers. Even though the vast majority of the information is objective, reporting entities are required to provide valuations of the features of the supply chain relationship. The information collected through the data pooling initiative can be matched with the seller's internal rating, which, because of the firm-specific nature of the risk and the competitive advantage it can represent for each trade credit financier, is not sharable.

---

[2]For a broader discussion on the validation of internal rating systems, see Tasche (2008).

The second application of credit risk measures in risk management is portfolio reporting by rating class and *CaR*. Reporting by capital allocation is particularly relevant for trade credit financiers, especially when it allows one to disentangle the contribution of the concentration of exposures with respect to *CaR* calculated as a portfolio invariant (Gordy 2003). A granularity adjustment for portfolio risk factors is therefore introduced in both industry models of VaR for credit risk and regulatory capital requirements, as in the following equation (Gordy and Luetkebohmert 2013):

$$GA = C \times H \times \sum_{i=1}^{n} EAD_i \qquad (2.2)$$

where

GA is the granularity adjustment of capital

H is the Herfindahl index, specified as $\dfrac{\left(\sum\limits_{i=1}^{n} EAD_1^2 \right)}{\left(\sum\limits_{i=1}^{n} EAD \right)^2}$

C is the proportionality constant, between 0.5 and 10 percent, depending on *LGD*, the *PD*, and correlation of defaults.

Table 2.4 shows an example of the reporting template based on the application of credit risk parameters for a European financier. The quarterly analysis allows one to assess the relation between the variation of *GA* and that of *CaR* for given levels of *H* as determined by the name concentration.

The bulk of the application of credit risk measures is represented by the management of credit with the following aims:

- Portfolio management
- Coordination of debtors' financing decisions

Table 2.4 Report on GA and CaR for a medium-sized factor

Quarter	EAD	H index	GA	GA/EAD	CaR
	Euro	%	Euro	%	Euro

Source: Author's elaboration.

From the trade credit financier's perspective, the application of the risk parameters to portfolio management means that the following strategic decisions are driven by credit risk measures:

- The target *CaR* for the portfolio of credit exposures. Generally, it is very important for trade credit financiers to define the target in light of the concentration issues. In particular, it is crucial for market trade credit financing solutions to define the target coherently with the rating level that the issue will target.
- Segmentation of the portfolio of credit exposures. The application of credit risk measures and *CaR* in this area is even more important for trade credit financiers compared with universal financiers, since the former finance a preexisting business relationship between the seller and a buyer and, therefore, the segmentation and its modifications can be constrained bringing to reduced diversification, thus it is compelling to anticipate future capital needs.
- Optimization of the credit portfolio through securitization, credit derivatives, and portfolio insurance. Because of the constrained capability in actively managing the portfolio segmentation, portfolio optimization is particularly important for trade credit financiers found to use securitization and portfolio insurance instruments (Jones 2010).

Regarding the coordination of financing decisions, the following are the main areas of the application of credit risk measures (De Laurentis 2001):

- Development and preservation of an effective credit discipline
- Activation of the review process
- Value creation by obtaining outstanding profitability conditions through pricing
- Management compensation

The introduction of common measures to compare and exchange outputs produced by different processes exposed to credit risk favors effective discipline. Moreover, since risk culture is considered critical in ensuring the stability of the financier (Group of Thirty 2013) through the maintenance of predefined standards, financial institutions affirm that credit risk measures reinforce credit culture, particularly after troubled times associated with relevant losses (Treacy and Carey 2000).

The relevance of the coordination is essential in the review process described in Credit Risk Origination section. In particular, ratings are not limited to information dissemination but promote action when market and/or firm development threatens to affect them (Boot, Milbourn, and Schmeits 2006). Given such a perspective, a scattered approach to the exposure review must be avoided, for that would lead to an excessive concentration of exposures in some rating classes at the expense of others, with loss of the meaningfulness of the ratings over time (Altman 1998).

Since their introduction, risk measures have been extensively applied to the area of risk-adjusted performance to foster value creation (Altman and Saunders 1998). Systems have been developed that regularly report on risk-adjusted returns on capital, with the aim of evaluating ex ante the capital to allocate to each business unit and measuring ex post the contribution of each business unit to value creation (Zaik et al. 1996) through a comparison between the cost of capital and the risk-adjusted performance of the trade credit financier. For trade credit financiers, total remuneration considers both the anticipation service and the guarantee for the default risk of the counterparty. If the trade credit financier is able to set the pricing of the services under the assumption that default risk and dilution risk are independent and *VaR* is subadditive, the risk-adjusted interest rate for advancing trade credits (i_r) and the risk-adjusted fee for the guarantee and management service (f_r) can be set as follows:

$$i_r = \frac{i_{rf} + (ELR + ELR_d) + (Var + Var_d) \times (k_e - i_{rf})}{1 - (ELR + ELR_d)} \qquad (2.3)$$

$$f_r = mc\% + ELR \qquad (2.4)$$

where
    i_{rf} is the risk-free rate
    k_e is the cost of capital of the trade credit financier
    $mc\%$ is the managing cost as a percentage of the nominal value of the receivable

ELR is the expected loss rate for default risk

ELR_d is the expected loss rate for dilution risk

VaR is the percentage value at risk for default risk

VaR_d is the percentage value at risk for dilution risk

In equation (2.3), ELR reflects the losses the trade credit financier can suffer for the following reasons:

- The default of both the trade debtor and the seller/assignor. For this reason, it is crucial for trade credit financiers to develop approaches to measure the correlation between the counterparties. Approaches developed for financial guarantors must be adapted, since the seller/assignor and the trade debtor are exposed to common risk factors through the supply chain (see Chapter 4);
- The manifestation of dilution risk. The risk source can hinder the trade credit financier from collecting either the advanced amount or the guaranteed amount of trade credit.

From equation (2.4), f_r is a function of the managing cost of the assigned/sold receivables as a percentage of the turnover of trade credit plus ELR. Obviously, diluted credits do not expose the financier to the risk of default of the trade debtor.

Nonetheless, the application of risk-adjusted interest rates and fees must be weighted in light of the following:

- Implausible pricing levels (Repullo and Suarez 2004)
- Pressure that the applications for profitability and pricing goals can be created directly on the system (Treacey and Carey 2000)
- The need to consider risk-adjusted performances more as a key reference than as a definitive rule to apply (De Laurentis 2001)

In conclusion, regarding the application of credit risk parameters to credit risk management processes, one must consider that its effectiveness is affected by the effort made by management, whose compensation, over the last years, has become increasingly sensitive to risk (Bai and Elyasiani 2013) in a way that should be compensated for taking exactly the risk desired by the board (Stulz 2008), thus reducing excess variability (Danielsson et al. 2002) and being accountable for the investor capital they put at risk (Zaik et al. 1996). In regard to trade credit financing activities, empirical evidence has shown that the higher the short-term intensity of investments, the greater the risk (Livne, Markarian, and Mironov 2013).

Within the scope of application of credit risk parameters, it is possible to outline a further area of utilization in the administration process. Credit risk administration applications of risk measures invest:

- Compliance with regulation and internal codes
- Balance sheet values
- Transparency

The need to be compliant with regulations requires the classification of counterparties into regulatory categories. The application of credit risk parameters can support such a process by ensuring consistency between the effective risk levels and the information conveyed to supervisors. In Europe, banks and branches residing within the European Union (EU) must be able to reconcile internal classes of the rating system with performing and nonperforming regulatory classes (European Commission, EU Regulation no. 227/2015). Table 2.5 presents the relation between the regulatory subcategories and the credit risk parameters that can be applied to classify exposures. In particular, for trade credit financiers, the separation between performing and nonperforming exposures can be based on the PD. Parameters above their trigger levels can reveal entry into nonperforming status, as opposed to temporary difficulties. Once in nonperforming status, the credit risk parameters can encourage the trade credit financier to separate past due exposures from unlikely to pay exposures. Specifically, even though the PD of the counterparty has not breached the trigger level, high ELR_d values can signal difficulties in commercial payments that should be carefully evaluated when the past dues are diffused across suppliers. Such signals can be particularly useful in deciding to extend forbearance measures to exposures expected to revert to performing status. Dilution parameters can help the trade credit financier evaluate if liquidity tensions are originating from particular types of contracts and/or sectors.

Table 2.5 The relationship between regulatory categories and credit risk parameters

Regulatory category	Regulatory subcategory	Credit risk parameter
Performing loans		PD, ELR_d
Nonperforming loans	Past due exposures. Material exposures, which are more than 90 days past due	PD, ELR_d, EAD
Nonperforming loans	Unlikely to pay exposures. The debtor is assessed as unlikely to pay its credit obligations in full without realization of collateral, regardless of the existence of any past due amount or of the number of days past due	PD, ELR_d, LGD
Nonperforming loans	Forborne exposures. Debt contracts in respect of which forbearance measures have been applied	PD, LGD

Source: Author's elaboration of EU Regulation n.227/2015.

Concerning the determination of balance sheet values, the application of credit risk parameters is instrumental to ensuring consistency between internal risk data and external communications. The expected risk values should be mirrored in the trade credit financier's provisioning policies, taking into account the impact of dilution risk as a source of credit risk. Nonperforming loans that do not pass the impairment test are characterized by expected recoveries lower than the balance sheet exposure; therefore, *LGD* will affect provisioning (Peter 2006). In light of the insignificant expected recoveries in the presence of dilution risk, the impairment test will determine the exposure's write-off.

More than supervisors, credit risk parameters can support the disclosure of useful information to a broad range of stakeholders with the aim of enhancing transparency (Linsey and Shrives 2006). In light of the modest and incomparable risk disclosures of firms (Lajili and Zeghal 2005), the Basel II Capital Accord introduced a set of information that must be reported annually. Trade credit financiers must comply with the general disclosure of risk management objectives and policies, including strategies and processes; the structure and organization of relevant risk management functions; the scope and nature of risk reporting and measurement systems; and policies for hedging and mitigating risks. Moreover, specific quantitative disclosure requirements were introduced for which the application of credit risk parameters can be useful:

- *EAD* by major types of exposure
- Geographic distribution of exposures
- Industry distribution of exposures
- Portfolio maturity
- Impaired loans by major industry, geographic area, and counterparty type
- Allowances by major industry, geographic area, and counterparty type and reconciliation with impaired loans
- For each portfolio, the amount of exposure (for internal rating–based banks, drawn plus *EAD* on the undrawn amount) by regulatory approach

More than the Basel Capital Accord, the application of credit risk parameters can help trade credit financiers to fulfill the disclosure requirements of International Financial Reporting Standard 7 (IFRS Foundation 2005, 1), aimed at requiring

> Entities to provide disclosures in their financial statements, that enable users to evaluate (1) the significance of financial instruments for the entity's financial position and performance; and (2) the nature and extent of risks arising from financial instruments to which the entity is exposed during the period and at the reporting date, and how the entity manages those risks.
> In particular, credit risk disclosure requirements concern

- Credit quality
- Collateral
- Loan performance

European financial institutions deliver the risk data using International Technical Standards. In particular, Common Reporting COREP standards are used for prudential reporting, while FINREP is for statistical

Table 2.6 Credit risk parameters for COREP reporting institutions

	Default rate (%)	Loss rate (%)	PD adj (%)	LGD (%)
Austria	1.95	31.60	2.02	29.73
Belgium	0.76	14.49	1.99	27.77
Bulgaria			3.66	39.57
Croatia	7.04	21.44	4.38	38.32
Cyprus			3.63	3.63
Czech	0.74	32.94	1.90	33.51
Denmark	0.66	16.58	1.57	22.31
Estonia			1.05	41.66
Finland	0.88		0.57	34.00
France	0.58	36.23	1.43	33.62
Germany	1.00	26.39	1.35	35.79
Greece			13.65	40.51
Hungary	0.39	43.41	2.19	39.83
Ireland	2.00	25.87	1.76	34.06
Italy	6.90	39.89	9.78	37.30
Latvia	1.84	59.28	1.81	42.44
Lithuania			1.36	41.19
Luxembourg	0.78	31.28	1.10	31.71
Malta			5.59	33.88
Netherlands	2.32	8.55	2.26	25.78
Norway	1.45	13.28	1.49	26.61
Poland	1.15	40.13	1.75	31.58
Portugal	3.12	34.39	6.72	41.81
Romania			3.34	38.13
Slovakia	1.98	67.62	1.77	39.94
Slovenia	1.94	32.64	7.95	40.69
Spain	3.18	28.38	8.52	40.32
Sweden	0.18	14.84	0.62	25.08
United Kingdom	1.24	15.48	1.03	34.21

Source: Author's elaboration of European Banking Authority data (2018).
Notes:
- The data are from the fourth quarter of 2017.
- The data are averages weighted by the number of reporting institutions.
- The loss rate and default rate are calculated from the reporting templates.

reporting (European Commission, Commission Implementing Regulation no. 680/2014). Concerning reporting on capital and risk, the following disclosure templates of COREP are supported by the application of the credit risk parameters:

- Credit and counterparty credit risks and free deliveries—standardized approach to capital requirements
- Credit and counterparty credit risks and free deliveries—internal rating–based approach to capital requirements
- Credit risk—equity, internal rating–based approaches to capital requirements
- Credit risk—securitization, standardized approach to capital requirements
- Credit risk—securitization, internal rating–based approach to capital requirements
- Credit risk—detailed information on securitizations by originators and sponsors

Table 2.6 shows the credit risk parameters by the country of the exposure counterparty for European reporting institutions under COREP. The empirical evidence shows that geography still matters in credit risk among European countries, where the final loss rate can be affected more by either the *PD* or the *LGD*.

Conclusions

The application of credit risk measures to trade credit financiers has been extended and can contribute significantly to value creation. In particular, because of the complexity of the risk management framework, embedding risk measures within credit risk control allows one to limit exposure in light of the risk from the seller/assignor–debtor pair and provide management with a comprehensive and updated information set to make decisions on maintained and transferred risks.

Over time, financial intermediaries have increased the applications of internal ratings to approve new financing, even though their relevance to lending decisions is affected by both the segment and creditor characteristics. The processes characterized by the most advanced applications of credit risk parameters pertain to the control area. Such applications are particularly valuable for trade credit financiers who can take advantage of the observation of high-frequency payments from commercial transactions.

The most promising application of credit risk measures is in the field of credit risk management, where the complexity of the risk management framework for trade credit financing can improve capital allocation and should foster value creation by adjusting performance measures and pricing in light of broader coverage of risk types and the effective origination of risks.

CHAPTER 3

Trade Credit Instruments in Capital Adequacy Regulation

Introduction

Starting in the late 1980s, financial intermediaries have had to comply with capital requirements based on recommendations developed by the Basel Committee on Banking Supervision. The worldwide adoption of these standards into domestic regulations currently involves more than 90 percent of global banking assets (Basel Committee on Banking Supervision 2017a). The final goal of ensuring the stability and soundness of the financial system has motivated the continuous review of these standards, leading to the evolution from Basel I to Basel III.[1] The evolution of standards has been accompanied by the progressive enlargement of the scope of application through country-level choices on the implementation of standards, extending applications from a consolidated, banking group level exclusively to include the individual financial intermediary level.

Trade credit financiers are part of the scope of the application of the Basel Capital Accords if they are a holding company of a banking group, a bank, or a financial company inside a banking group. According to the standards, trade credit affects the capital requirements for credit risk, with a potential mitigating role. Generally, in line with multiple managerial approaches, many options are introduced for the regulatory treatment of trade credit financing exposures. The determination of capital requirements for credit risk is based on risk weights

---

[1] This chapter considers the regulatory standards as being implemented or coming into force by 2019.

(see Credit Risk Capital Requirements: A Holistic View section), calculated according to different rules, between a standardized methodology (see Trade Credit Financing Instruments under the Standardized Methodology section) and an internal ratings–based (IRB) methodology (see Trade Credit Financing Instruments under the IRB Methodology section). The treatment of exposures originated from trade credit financing differs in the rules for exposure in the standardized methodology (see Trade Credit Financing Instruments under the Standardized Methodology section) and those based on purchased trade credits (see Exposures Based on Purchased Trade Credits section) and collateralized by trade credits (see Exposures Collateralized by Trade Credits section) in the IRB methodology. Lastly, because minimum capital requirements do not address single name concentration risk, trade credit financiers must comply with large exposure standards (see Capital Regulation on Large Exposures section). The chapter ends with brief conclusions on the application of the prudential regulation to trade credit financiers (see Conclusions section).

Credit Risk Capital Requirements: A Holistic View

According to the regulatory framework, capital adequacy is based on minimum capital requirements calculated according to standard rules (Pillar 1), whose reliability with respect to the specificities of the intermediary is assessed by the supervisory authority (Pillar 2) and, through the disclosure of relevant information, the market assesses whether the minimum capital requirements provided are adequate with respect to the risks assumed (Pillar 3).

Under the Basel Capital Accords, the minimum capital requirement for credit risk (CR) is calculated as follows:

$$CR = \frac{RC}{TRWA} \geq 8\% \tag{3.1}$$

where

RC is regulatory capital

$TRWA$ is total risk-weighted assets (RWA) for credit risk

For each exposure, the credit *RWA* are calculated as the product of the exposure (E) and the risk weight (W). The Basel Capital Accords provide two methods for determining the weight to apply to each exposure[2]:

- The standardized methodology, which includes the simplified standardized methodology
- The IRB methodology

The standardized methodology is targeted at financial intermediaries whose risk management systems are not very sophisticated, to produce estimates of losses to also be used for regulatory purposes. Within this methodology, the exposure E is equal to that recorded in the financial statements. In the spirit of achieving greater capital requirement sensitivity with respect to effective risk, the Basel Committee has stated that, where available, the weight is determined based on ratings issued by external credit assessment institutions recognized by the supervisory authority, first, of all the rating agencies.

In an attempt to differentiate the weights more on the basis of credit risk, the Basel Committee has provided mappings between external ratings and weights in relation to the institutional typology of the counterparty considered, as indicated in Table 3.1.

The issue of guarantees is addressed among the risk mitigation techniques. In terms of collateral, the standardized methodology provides for the application of lower weights for:

- Real estate
- Gold and cash
- Qualified transferable securities

Furthermore, exposures backed by personal guarantees and credit derivatives benefit from replacing the weight of the principal with that of the guarantor/seller of protection in the case of a better assessment of creditworthiness, if the latter is

---

[2]This chapter does not cover the regulatory treatment of securitization exposure.

Table 3.1 Risk weights (W) in the standardized methodology

Category of the exposure	Credit assessment						
	AAA/AA-	A+/A-	BBB+/BBB-	BB+/BB-	B+/B-	Below B-	Unrated
Supervised banks and securities firms (Option 1)	20%	50%	100%	100%	100%	150%	100%
Supervised banks and securities firms (Option 2)	20%	50%	50%	150%	150%	150%	50%
Maturity shorter than 3 months	20%	20%	20%	50%	50%	150%	20%
Sovereigns	0%	20%	50%	100%	100%	150%	100%
Noncentral government public sector entities	20%	50%	100%	100%	100%	150%	100%
Corporates	20%	50%	100%	100%	150%	150%	100%
Retail portfolio				75%			

Source: Basel Committee on Banking Supervision (2006).

- A sovereign state, a public entity, a supervised financial intermediary
- A corporate entity with an external rating of at least A−

The last type of risk mitigation technique allowed by the Basel Capital Accords is netting, which then determines the decrease in exposure. The netting agreement must have a solid legal basis and the risks that can alter its effectiveness must be properly monitored.

The effect of external ratings on weights is insignificant when the exposure has expired and is to a counterparty in default.[3] In the absence of guarantees and regardless of the type of counterparty, the weight notably becomes 150 percent, requiring an increase in the regulatory capital to be held by the financial intermediary that is 50 percent higher than the maximum for an exposure not assigned an external, unsecured rating.

Within the standardized methodology, a simplified approach is introduced, the simplified standardized methodology, which includes all the simplest options. For example, the weights are assigned without considering the possibility of an external rating. The ease of application of this methodology and the elemental nature of the rules make this an affordable option for small financial intermediaries that are not particularly exposed to credit risk.

For the most sophisticated financial intermediaries in the management of credit risk, the Basel Capital Accords provide the IRB methodology. Here, the *RWAs* are determined based on the internal data of the intermediary on the actual losses incurred, estimating the expected loss. The extent of use of internal data to calculate minimum capital requirements is a function of the degree of sophistication of the credit risk management system. The following two approaches are introduced for this purpose:

- A foundation approach
- An advanced approach

---

[3]For a broader discussion of the default definition under the Basel Capital Accords, see Probability of Default section in Chapter 1.

The Basel Capital Accords do not allow intermediaries to determine the *RWAs* on the basis of their portfolio models in the *VaR* logic, but, depending on the approach, financial intermediaries are authorized to estimate the expected values of the variables that determine the losses, that is, *PD, LGD, EAD*, and *M*. To estimate *PD, LGD, EAD*, and *M* in the advanced approach, intermediaries must be authorized by the supervisory authority that issues the validation to use the foundation approach, where the internal estimate is limited to the *PD* and regulatory estimates are used for the other parameters.

The estimates of these risk parameters are then included in a regulatory function based on Merton's (1974) original credit portfolio model and then adapted to obtain an asymptotic single-risk factor model (Vasicek 2002), assuming the portfolio's infinite granularity and a single systemic risk factor in order to ensure that the weight of each exposure is unaffected by the portfolio composition (Gordy 2003). Therefore, the Basel Committee has determined a capital absorption of *k* percent within a *VaR* model. For each exposure, the *RWA* variable is determined as follows:

$$RWA = 12.5 \times k\% \times EAD \qquad (3.2)$$

Similar to the standardized methodology, the credit risk of the counterparties differs according to the institutional category that determines the allocation of exposures to one of the regulatory portfolios, as shown in Figure 3.1.

The regulatory function that transforms the estimates of the risk parameters into *k* percent differs according to the regulatory portfolio considered. Figure 3.2 shows the simulation of the weights for large, medium-sized, and small enterprises when the *PD* changes using the *LGD* and *M* regulatory estimates.

With regard to risk mitigation techniques, the financial intermediaries applying the IRB methodology exploit a widening of the guarantees admitted in decreasing *W*. In addition to the risk mitigation tools of the standardized methodology, trade receivables and certain types of goods and properties also have a negative impact on *W*. With regard to

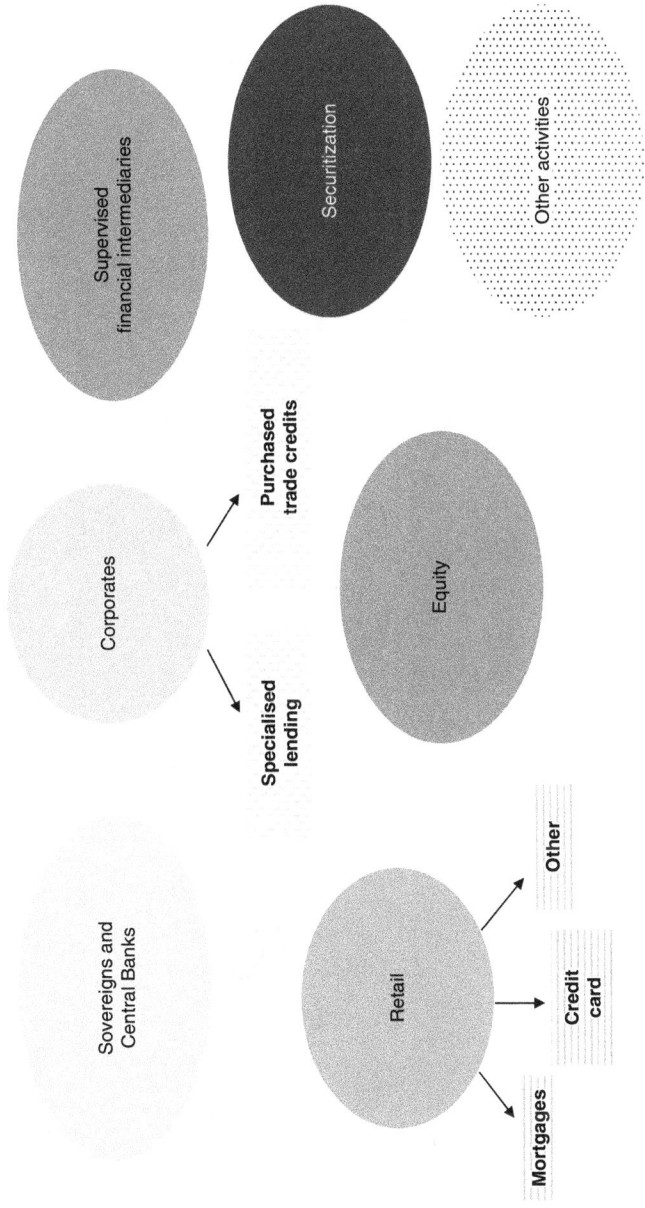

Figure 3.1 *Regulatory portfolios under the IRB approach*

Source: Author's elaboration.

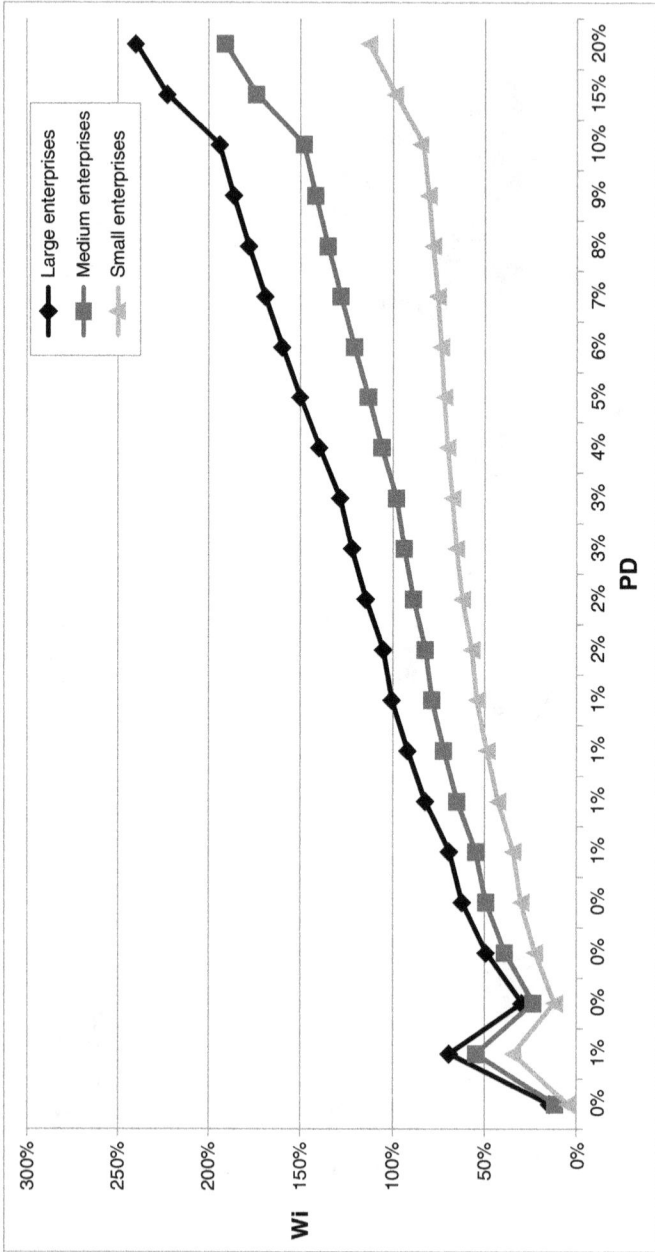

Figure 3.2 Simulation of W by the PD and regulatory estimates of LGD and M

Source: Author's elaboration.

Notes:

LGD = 45%

M = 1

defaulted exposures, the IRB methodology confirms the definition introduced in the standardized methodology and k percent is determined as the difference between the exposure to the event of default and the best *LGD* forecast.

Trade Credit Financing Instruments under the Standardized Methodology

The Basel Capital Accords do not provide any specific treatment for the financing of trade receivables in the standardized methodology. Considering the structure and characteristics of trade credit financing exposure without recourse to the seller, it is possible to hypothesize, by analogy, the extension of the risk mitigation specifications. Among these, the treatment is presumably aligned to guarantees, because trade credits are not acknowledged as financial collaterals. For them to qualify as personal credit risk mitigation, the following operational requirements are introduced (Basel Committee on Banking Supervision 2006, 46–48):

- The guarantee must be direct, explicit, unconditional, and irrevocable.
- The following are eligible guarantors:
  - Sovereign states, public entities not belonging to central government, banks, and investment firms with a weighting lower than that of the principal.
  - Other subjects with a rating equal to or better than A–. The guarantees of the parent company are also considered.

In the presence of operational requirements, trade credit financing exposures with recourse can be assumed to be partly included in the framework described, based on the following assumptions: If the exposure counterparty is recognized as the assigned debtor, then, according to the rules for personal guarantees, the weighting of the assigned debtor can be replaced by that of the assignor, who, contractually, retains the risk of the transaction against the assignee. Therefore, in case the assignor is less risky than the trade debtor, the calculation of *RWA* would be

$$RWA = E \times W_a \qquad (3.3)$$

where
    E is the exposure
    W_a is the risk weight of the assignor when it is lower than the risk weight of the trade debtor.

The calculation of *RWA* for nonrecourse assignments is based on the creditworthiness of the trade debtor. Therefore, it can be obtained as follows:

$$RWA = E \times W_d \qquad (3.4)$$

where E is the exposure; W_d is the risk weight of the trade debtor.

In terms of risk sources, the standardized methodology does not introduce an explicit treatment for dilution risk.

Trade Credit Financing Instruments under the IRB Methodology

The IRB methodology explicitly provides that the sources of risk for transactions involving the purchase of receivables are represented by

- The risk of default
- The risk of dilution

The Basel Capital Accords provide under this methodology an additional option for trade credit financing exposures, represented by a treatment to estimate the risk parameters for single exposure (bottom up) or for pools of exposures (top down). Further, trade receivables are recognized as an eligible financial guarantee, with positive effects on the determination of capital requirements. Roughly, the options for the treatment of trade credit financing exposures for default risk can be classified as follows:

- Bottom-up treatment of trade credits as risk exposure. Under this treatment, trade credits represent the risk exposure when the assignment is classified as a true sale. The calculation of the capital requirement can be determined according to either the foundation or the advanced approach.
- Top-down treatment of trade credits as risk exposure. Under this treatment, trade credits represent the risk exposure when they are managed in a pool, even though the assignment is not classified as a true sale. The calculation of the capital requirement can be determined according to either the foundation or the advanced approach.
- Treatment of trade receivables as collateral. Under this treatment, eligible trade credits mitigate the exposure to the seller/assignor. The calculation of the capital requirement can be determined according to either the foundation or the advanced approach.

For dilution risk, unless the bank can demonstrate to its supervisor that the risk is immaterial, the following options are introduced for the measurement of capital requirements:

- Bottom-up treatment of trade credits. Under this treatment, capital requirements for dilution risk are calculated at the debtor level.
- Top-down treatment of trade credits. Under this treatment, capital requirements are calculated at the pool level.

Exposures Based on Purchased Trade Credits

The bottom-up treatment of trade receivables applies to both retail and corporate portfolios. In terms of default risk, under the foundation approach, the intermediary determines the capital requirement using an internal estimate of the PD and the regulatory estimates of the other risk parameters. For corporate receivables, the following parameters hold:

- Internal estimate of the probability of default of the trade debtor or the guarantor if lower (PD)
- Regulatory estimate of LGD, equal to 45 percent
- Regulatory estimate of M, equal to 2.5 years

- *EAD* equal to the outstanding credit/advance, that is, balance sheet exposure, plus 75 percent of any irrevocable revolving commitment to purchase credits, net of the capital requirement for dilution risk

The *RWA* for default risk for corporate debtors can be calculated according to the following equation:

$$RWA = 12.5 \times \left(EAD - k_d\%\right) \times k\% \qquad (3.5)$$

where

$$k\% = \left(45\% \times \Phi\left(\left(\frac{\Phi^{-1}(PD)}{\sqrt{1-R}}\right) + \left(\sqrt{\frac{R}{1-R}}\,\Phi^{-1}(0.999)\right)\right) - PD \times 45\%\right)$$

$$\times \frac{\left(1 + (M - 2.5) \times b(PD)\right)}{\left(1 - 1.5 \times b(PD)\right)}$$

$$R = 0.12 \times \frac{\left(1 - e^{-50PD}\right)}{\left(1 - e^{-50}\right)} + 0.24 \times \left(1 - \frac{\left(1 - e^{-50PD}\right)}{\left(1 - e^{-50}\right)}\right)$$

If the total sales of the counterparty are less than 50 million euros, *R* must be substituted with R_{SME}:

$$R_{SME} = 0.12 \times \frac{\left(1 - e^{-50PD}\right)}{\left(1 - e^{-50}\right)} + 0.24 \times \left(1 - \frac{\left(1 - e^{-50PD}\right)}{\left(1 - e^{-50}\right)}\right) - 0.04 \times \left(1 - \frac{(S - 5)}{45}\right)$$

$$b = \left(0.08451 - 0.05898 Ln(PD)\right)^2$$

$M = 2.5$ years

Under the advanced approach, the financial intermediary can use internal estimates of the risk parameters. In particular, *M* cannot be less than 1 year.

Dilution risk capital requirements are calculated at the debtor level, based on the following parameters:

- EL_d, equal to *PD*.
- LGD_d, equal to 100 percent.
- EAD_d, equal to the balance sheet exposure.
- An appropriate *M*. If the financial intermediary can demonstrate that the dilution risk is appropriately monitored and managed, to

be resolved within 1 year, the supervisor could allow the bank to apply a 1-year maturity.

Consequently, following from equation (3.5), RWA_d for dilution risk can be calculated as follows:

$$RWA_d = 12.5 \times EAD \times k_d\% \tag{3.6}$$

where

$$k_d\% = \left(100\% \times \Phi\left(\left(\frac{\Phi^{-1}(ELR_d)}{\sqrt{1-R}}\right) + \left(\sqrt{\frac{R}{1-R}}\Phi^{-1}(0.9999)\right)\right) - \right.$$

$$\left. ELR_d \times 100\%\right) \times \frac{(1 + (M - 2.5) \times b(ELR_d))}{(1 - 1.5 \times b(ELR_d))}$$

$$R = 0.12 \times \frac{(1 - e^{-50PD})}{(1 - e^{-50})} + 0.24 \times \left(1 - \frac{(1 - e^{-50PD})}{(1 - e^{-50})}\right)$$

$$b = (0.08451 - 0.05898Ln(PD))^2$$

M = appropriate maturity

The marginal relevance of each receivable in the total portfolio of purchased trade credits can lead the trade credit financier to exploit the application of the option of the top-down treatment. The following are the eligibility requirements for corporate trade receivables (Basel Committee on Banking Supervision 2006, 58–59):

- The receivables are purchased from unrelated, third-party sellers.
- The receivables are generated on an arm's-length basis between the seller and the obligor.
- The purchasing bank has a claim on all proceeds from the pool of receivables or a pro rata interest in the proceeds.
- The receivables do not originate from concentrated exposures.

Provided the purchasing bank complies with the IRB rules for retail exposure, purchased retail receivables are eligible for the top-down approach, as permitted within the standards for retail exposure.

Under the top-down foundation approach, the calculation of RWA for the default risk of corporate receivables is based on the following parameter estimations:

- *PD* equals *ELR* divided by *LGD*.
- *LGD* equals 40 percent.
- *EAD* equals the balance sheet exposure plus 40 percent of any irrevocable revolving purchasing agreement.

The calculation of *RWA* for the default risk of corporate receivables is as follows:

$$RWA = 12.5 \times EAD \times (1 - k_d\%) \times k\% \qquad (3.7)$$

where

$$k\% = \left(45\% \times \Phi\left(\left(\frac{\Phi^{-1}(PD)}{\sqrt{1-R}} \right) + \left(\sqrt{\frac{R}{1-R}} \Phi^{-1}(0.999) \right) \right) - PD \times 45\% \right) \times$$

$$\frac{\left(1 + (M - 2.5) \times b(PD)\right)}{\left(1 - 1.5 \times b(PD)\right)}$$

$$R_{SME} = 0.12 \times \frac{\left(1 - e^{-50PD}\right)}{\left(1 - e^{-50}\right)} + 0.24 \times \left(1 - \frac{\left(1 - e^{-50PD}\right)}{\left(1 - e^{-50}\right)}\right)$$

$$- 0.04 \times \left(1 - \frac{(S - 5)}{45}\right)$$

$$b = \left(0.08451 - 0.05898Ln(PD)\right)^2$$

M = maturity of the portfolio that can be no less than 1 year

The calculation of *RWA* for the default risk of retail receivables follows the supervisory equation for an "Other retail" portfolio:

$$RWA = 12.5 \times EAD \times (1 - k_d\%) \times k\% \qquad (3.8)$$

where

$$k\% = \left(LGD \times \Phi\left(\left(\frac{\Phi^{-1}(PD)}{\sqrt{1-R}} \right) + \left(\sqrt{\frac{R}{1-R}}\Phi^{-1}(0.9999) \right) \right) - PD \times LGD \right)$$

$$R = 0.03 \times \frac{\left(1 - e^{-35PD}\right)}{\left(1 - e^{-35}\right)} + 0.16\left(1 - \frac{\left(1 - e^{-35PD}\right)}{\left(1 - e^{-35}\right)} \right)$$

The recurrence of a guarantee mitigating risk can justify the substitution of the *PD* estimated for the pool with the guarantor's *PD*.

Such a top-down option allows for corporate receivables to move to the advanced approach only by being able to produce an internal estimate of either the *PD* or the *LGD* of the pool. It is important to recognize that the *LGD* used for the IRB capital calculation for purchased receivables cannot be less than the long-run default-weighted average loss rate given default. Since the calculation of the *RWA* is involved, internal estimation of the credit conversion factor of a revolving purchase agreement is not permitted. Therefore, equation (3.9) yields

$$RWA = 12.5 \times EAD \times \left(1 - k_d\%\right) \times k\% \qquad (3.9)$$

where

$$k\% = \left(LGD \times \Phi\left(\left(\frac{\Phi^{-1}(PD)}{\sqrt{1-R}} \right) + \left(\sqrt{\frac{R}{1-R}}\Phi^{-1}(0.9999) \right) \right) \right.$$
$$\left. - PD \times LGD \right) \times \frac{\left(1 + (M - 2.5) \times b(PD)\right)}{\left(1 - 1.5 \times b(PD)\right)}$$

$$R_{SME} = 0.12 \times \frac{\left(1 - e^{-50PD}\right)}{\left(1 - e^{-50}\right)} + 0.24 \times \left(1 - \frac{\left(1 - e^{-50PD}\right)}{\left(1 - e^{-50}\right)} \right) - 0.04 \times \left(1 - \frac{(S - 5)}{45} \right)$$

$$b = \left(0.08451 - 0.05898Ln(PD)\right)^2$$

M = maturity of the portfolio, which cannot be less than 1 year

Concerning dilution risk, a common approach is proposed. The calculation of RWA_d is therefore expressed by the following formula, at pool level:

$$RWA_d = 12.5 \times EAD \times k_d\% \qquad (3.10)$$

where

$$k_d\% = \left(100\% \times \Phi\left(\left(\frac{\Phi^{-1}(ELR_d)}{\sqrt{1-R}}\right) + \left(\sqrt{\frac{R}{1-R}}\Phi^{-1}(0.9999)\right)\right)\right.$$

$$\left. - ELR_d \times 100\%\right) \times \frac{\left(1+(M-2.5)\times b(ELR_d)\right)}{\left(1-1.5\times b(ELR_d)\right)}$$

$$R = 0.12 \times \frac{\left(1-e^{-50PD}\right)}{\left(1-e^{-50}\right)} + 0.24 \times \left(1 - \frac{\left(1-e^{-50PD}\right)}{\left(1-e^{-50}\right)}\right)$$

$$b = \left(0.08451 - 0.05898 Ln(PD)\right)^2$$

M = appropriate maturity

Exposures Collateralized by Trade Credits

In the IRB foundation approach, the Basel Committee expands the range of eligible collaterals for the determination of LGD. The additional financial collaterals allowed in the IRB foundation approach compared to the standard methodology (other eligible IRB collateral) encompass trade receivables. Trade receivables must comply with the following requirements to be considered qualified IRB collateral (Basel Committee on Banking Supervision 2006, 112–13):

- The value of the portfolio of receivables must be equal to 125 percent of the exposure, corresponding to a maximum advance of 80 percent of the transferred portfolio of trade receivables.
- The creditor must be certain of being able to dispose of trade receivables in case of insolvency of the debtor.

- The intermediary must assess the credit risk associated with trade receivables as part of a robust process, considering the following:
  - The sector to which the debtor and the debtor's customers belong
  - An adequate ratio between the advanced and transferred portfolios, with the consideration of dilution risk
  - A continuous monitoring process, particularly for heavily concentrated portfolios
- Adequate diversification of the transferred portfolio and low correlation with the debtor counterpart are necessary.

The qualification of trade receivables under operational requirements allows the trade credit financier to apply a lower LGD, that is, 35 percent; therefore, RWA in the foundation approach is determined as follows:

$$RWA = 12.5 \times EAD \times k\% \qquad (3.11)$$

$$k\% = \left(35\% \times \Phi\left(\left(\frac{\Phi^{-1}(PD)}{\sqrt{1-R}} \right) + \left(\sqrt{\frac{R}{1-R}} \Phi^{-1}(0.9999) \right) \right) \right)$$

$$- PD \times 35\% \right) \times \frac{\left(1 + (M - 2.5) \times b(PD)\right)}{\left(1 - 1.5 \times b(PD)\right)}$$

$$R = 0.12 \times \frac{\left(1 - e^{-50PD}\right)}{\left(1 - e^{-50}\right)} + 0.24 \times \left(1 - \frac{\left(1 - e^{-50PD}\right)}{\left(1 - e^{-50}\right)}\right)$$

If the total sales of the counterparty are less than 50 million euros, R must be substituted with R_{SME}:

$$R_{SME} = 0.12 \times \frac{\left(1 - e^{-50PD}\right)}{\left(1 - e^{-50}\right)} + 0.24 \times \left(1 - \frac{\left(1 - e^{-50PD}\right)}{\left(1 - e^{-50}\right)}\right) - 0.04 \times \left(1 - \frac{(S - 5)}{45}\right)$$

$$b = \left(0.08451 - 0.05898 Ln(PD)\right)^2$$

$$M = 2.5 \text{ years}$$

Because k percent is linear with respect to LGD, the opportunity to apply a reduced risk parameter leads to an equal reduction in the capital requirement, all else being equal.

In the advanced approach, the trade credit financier can increase regulatory capital savings, depending on the trade credit financier's own estimates of LGD, EAD, and M.

On the dilution risk side, such an option does not introduce a capital requirement, but it is part of the operational requirements in the risk analysis.

Capital Regulation on Large Exposures

The minimum capital requirements discussed in Credit Risk Capital Requirements: A Holistic View section are not designed specifically to protect financial intermediaries from large losses resulting from the sudden default of a single counterparty or connected counterparties. Therefore, the Basel Committee on Banking Supervision finalized a new standard that will come into force in 2019.[4]

A large exposure is defined as the sum of all of a financial intermediary's exposures to a counterparty or to a group of connected counterparties exceeding 10 percent of the intermediary's eligible capital. Financial intermediaries must report the following:

- All exposures equal to or above 10 percent of the eligible capital.
- All other exposures, with or without the effect of credit risk mitigation being taken into account, equal to or above 10 percent of the bank's eligible capital.
- All exempted exposures with values equal to or above 10 percent of the bank's eligible capital (i.e., exposures to sovereigns, banks, covered bonds).
- Their largest 20 exposures to counterparties included in the scope of application, irrespective of their values relative to the bank's eligible capital base.

---

[4]Basel Committee on Banking Supervision (2014).

The minimum capital requirement for large exposures is determined according to the following equation:

$$\sum_{i=1}^{n} LE_i \leq 25\% RC \qquad (3.12)$$

where
LE_i is a large generic exposure i
RC is regulatory capital

Equation (3.12) is intended for both independent and connected counterparties. The connectedness between the counterparties is evaluated based on the following criteria:

- Control relationship. One of the counterparties has direct or indirect control over the other. Such control can derive from holding more than 50 percent of voting rights; voting agreements; significant influence over the appointment or dismissal of an entity's administrative, management, or supervisory body; and a controlling influence over senior management due to contractual agreements.

- Economic interdependence. If one of the counterparties were to experience financial problems, in particular, funding or repayment difficulties, the other would consequently also be likely to encounter funding or repayment difficulties.

Because of the financing relationships in the supply chain, the classification criteria of economic interdependence are particularly relevant to trade credit financiers. According to the Basel Committee on Banking Supervision (2014), the following situations must be evaluated in the detection of economic interdependence:

- Fifty percent or more of one counterparty's gross receipts or gross expenditures (on an annual basis) is derived from transactions with the other counterparty (e.g., the owner of a residential/commercial property and the tenant who pays a significant part of the rent).

- One counterparty has fully or partly guaranteed the exposure of the other counterparty or is liable by other means and the exposure is so significant that the guarantor is likely to default if a claim arises.
- A significant part of one counterparty's production/output that cannot easily be replaced by other customers is sold to another counterparty.
- The expected source of funds to repay each loan one counterparty makes to another is the same and the counterparty does not have another source of income from which the loan could be fully repaid.
- It is likely that the financial problems of one counterparty would cause difficulties for the other counterparties in terms of the full and timely repayment of liabilities.
- The insolvency or default of one counterparty is likely to be associated with the insolvency or default of the other.
- Two or more counterparties rely on the same source for the majority of their funding and, in the event of the common provider's default, an alternative provider cannot be found. In this case, the funding problems of one counterparty are likely to spread to another due to one- or two-way dependence on the same main funding source.

The exposure to calculate LE_i is taken from the balance sheet and credit mitigation techniques can affect it as follows:

- Eligible collaterals modify the original exposure by the amount recognized for risk-based capital requirement purposes.
- Guarantees modify the counterparty for the guaranteed part of the exposure.

The potential impact of regulatory standards on trade credit financing can be particularly severe due to the nonqualification of trade receivables among credit mitigation techniques. In light of the findings on concentration measures and risk (see Chapter 1), not considering sectorial and geographical concentration can contribute to finding an excessive capital burden in the face of effective risk. Moreover, the criteria for the detection of economic interdependence risks including most supply chain relationships are not homogeneous in terms of relevant effects in the propagation of distress (see Chapter 4).

Conclusions

Trade credit financing exposures attract the application of capital requirements, depending on the underlying credit risk. The great flexibility of trade credits in being financed through several financial instruments is addressed through multiple regulatory capital treatment options intended to foster the convergence of capital requirements and economic capital. Nonetheless, the extent of such an alignment depends on the capital treatment option.

Under the standardized methodology, trade credits receive weak recognition in terms of risk mitigation, limited to exploiting the framework for the treatment of personal guarantees. Such a limitation can be particularly serious in light of the issues outlined in the application of the default definition in trade credit financing opportunities. Omission of an ad hoc treatment for trade credits justifies the absence of requirements for dilution risk.

In the IRB methodology, trade credit financing exposures are addressed through multiple options inside ordinary approaches. The capital treatment of purchased receivables is differentiated depending on the features of the asset pools. Therefore, trade credit financiers can choose between a bottom-up and a top-down approach. The effectiveness of the approaches in mitigating credit risk capital requirements depends on the type and credit quality of the trade debtors. Moreover, the future implementation of the revised version of the Basel III Accord will allow a reduced regulatory LGD in the top-down approach.[5] Regardless of the approach, dilution risk deserves an ad hoc capital treatment if the trade credit financier is unable to demonstrate the immateriality of the risk. Recourse exposures characterized by the management of trade credits like collateral can benefit from a significant reduction in the regulatory estimation of LGD; moreover, dilution risk is addressed through a monitoring standard.

---

[5]Basel Committee on Banking Supervision (2017b).

CHAPTER 4

Risk Mitigation of Trade Credit and Distress along the Supply Chain

An Empirical Analysis for the U.S. Market

Introduction

The previous chapters have placed great emphasis on the credit risk mitigating role of trade credits from the perspective of financiers. Nonetheless, trade credits originate from business relationships and, more recently, a distinct role in coordinating supply chains has been identified for trade credit. The impact on the other members is influenced by counterparty exposure, the structure of the industry in which the supply chain interactions take place, and the type of sector. Notwithstanding the relevance of the topic, little is known about the features of interfirm networks in the propagation and redistribution of the effects of financial distress among directly connected members (see Literature Background section). Because trade credit uses vary from country to country, the data are for the United States (see Data section), where trade credit traditionally represents the single most important source of short-term finance for enterprises (Petersen and Rajan 1997) and is among the most relevant trade finance markets for financial institutions (Factors Chain International 2016), with a stable pattern of year-end trade credit over time (U.S. Census Bureau 2016). Moreover, supply chains involve international business relationships, since imports of goods historically far outweigh exports (Bureau of Economic Analysis, Department of Commerce, U.S. International Trade in Goods and Services, 2016). The methodology is based on the informative relevance of supply chain relationships for external evaluators and the support of growth (see Methodology section). The results of the empirical analysis on the impact of distress in the supply chain on trade credit policy, risk, performance, and the financing choices of growth are presented in Empirical Results section. Concluding remarks are addressed in Conclusions section.

Literature Background

Recently a distinctive role for trade credit was identified as a mechanism to coordinate supply chains (Luo and Zhang 2012) that are targeted to optimize the flow of goods, information, and financial flows in inter- and intracompany boundaries in the market (Lambert, Cooper and Pagh 1998) in front of market changes (Stevens 1989). The presence of market power along the supply chain can impact the efficiency goal, affecting the distribution of the enhanced total performance among the members (Crook and Combs 2007): focal companies of a supply chain, being very often large and powerful, can impose their payment terms onto smaller companies, which in turn enforce their terms onto those smaller yet (Van Horen 2007. Empirical evidences show that the supply chain affects the financial performance of the members (Yu 2013): successful supply chains, featured by effective sourcing strategies, usage of information technology, integration and external relationships (D'Avanzo, Lewinski, and Van Wassenhove 2003), are associated with lower default risk (Ellinger et al. 2011), while supply chain disruption events can determine negative wealth and profitability outcomes for the member's investors both in the short term (Hendricks and Singhal 2003) and in the long term (Hendricks and Singhal 2005). Financial distress of suppliers has become a major concern for disruptions to normal activities (Kleindorfer and Saad 2005): financial distress by a supplier is found to affect other members of the supply chain, even though the impact is influenced by the counterparty exposure, the structure of the industry where supply chain interactions take place, and the type of sector. Given the financial distress of a firm, the strategies of the other members in supply interactions can determine the following effects: predation, because the competing nondistressed firms try to gain the monopoly resulting in further hurting of the distressed entity and benefiting the common supplier; bail out of the distressed entity through the supplier's concessions determining negative outcomes for all the members out of the distressed debtor; abetment, when the supplier decides to profit more from the nondistressed entity, with negative impact on the distressed entity (Yang, Birge, and Parker 2015). Depending on the selected strategy, the supply chain member can be exposed to counterparty risk toward the distressed entity: due to the high relative amount of trade credit extended, the ongoing business of a supply chain entity can be impaired by the bankruptcy of a relevant borrower and losses are determined by both credit exposure in the balance sheet and the reduction of future earnings if the customer is not replaced quickly, showing possible future impact on creditor's financial distress in the case of high leverage (Jorion and Zhang 2009); moreover, it can drive to the potential activation of chain effects (Kiyotaki and Moore 1997) that can pass liquidity shocks both upstream (Boissay and Gropp 2013 and downstream to other entities (Yang 2011). The outcomes of counterparty risk stemming from strategic decisions on the supply chain interactions with the distressed entity are affected by intraindustry relationships: multisourcing strategies inside the industry are ineffective when default dependence levels among suppliers are found significant due to the contagion (Wagner, Bode, and Koziol 2008) that is expected to be more relevant in concentrated industries (Lang and Stulz 1992). Moreover, the concentration level affects the spreading of contagion both in the suppliers' and customers' distressed entity industries (Hertzel et al. 2008). The magnitude of the propagation of shocks along the supply chain can be affected by the credit linkage among industries: empirical evidences show that the increase of direct trade credit relationships among industries significantly increases the output correlation, while an increase of bank credit related to trade credit is able to reduce the sectors' comovements. Moreover, the comovements among sectors deriving from trade credit usage can manifest also through links mediated by other industries (Raddatz 2010). Limited empirical evidences are available on cross-sectional determinants. The suppliers and customers of firms of unique or specialized products are expected to be strongly affected by the distress of the supply chain member (Titman and Wessels 1998).

Data

The sample considers all firms in the United States disclosing entry into bankruptcy proceedings through EDGAR filings that are not classified as financial intermediaries and whose data provider, Thomson Eikon, is able to collect information about the customers and suppliers connected with the defaulted entity through a value supply chain relationship. The final sample encompasses 146 corporations that went bankrupt between 2012 and 2016 (Table 4.1).[1]

Table 4.1 Defaulted firms' sample

	2012	2013	2014	2015	2016	Overall
Defaults	13	6	17	37	73	146
Percentage of relevant suppliers and customers	46.15	50.00	64.71	51.35	54.79	54.11
Relevant suppliers	4	3	15	31	78	131
Relevant customers	23	3	36	58	162	282

Source: Thomson Eikon data processed by the author.

Around 54 percent of the sample has information about at least one relevant customer and one supplier, and only 20 percent of the firms have only one relevant commercial counterparty. Firms with larger supply chain networks have up to 15 directly connected entities (suppliers or customers) and the total number of relevant customers is doubled with respect to suppliers (282 and 131, respectively).

A control sample for the analysis is constructed using industry sector matching for the suppliers and customers of the defaulted entities. The sample thus comprises all firms in the United States in the same sector from 2012 to 2016 (Table 4.2).

As expected, the most represented sector in the whole sample is manufacturing, and the control sample for the suppliers is more than 50 times the size of the default-related sample, while the customers' control sample is more than 35 times the size of the original sample. Moreover, the information sector shows the lowest incidence of defaulted supply relationships

---

[1]Thomson Eikon's value chain database includes customer and supplier relationships such as those reported in EDGAR filings and integrated with newsfeeds. Moreover, a confidence score is obtained with a minimum trigger value of 20 percent to detect a valid supply chain relationship. Relationships with financial intermediaries are not considered.

Table 4.2 Defaulted entities and control sample

NAICS sector	Suppliers' sample			Customers' sample		
	All	Connected with defaulted entities	Control	All	Connected with defaulted entities	Control
Accommodation and food service	139	2	137	–	–	–
Arts, entertainment, and recreation	92	1	91	94	3	91
Construction	156	1	155	158	3	155
Health care and social assistance	145	2	143	147	4	143
Information	1,099	9	1,090	1,108	18	1,090
Management of companies and enterprises	–	–	–	3	1	2
Manufacturing	1,577	51	1,526	3,093	111	2,982
Mining, quarrying, and oil and gas extraction	976	14	962	988	26	962
Other services	–	–	–	34	1	33
Professional, scientific, and technical service	974	14	960	978	18	960
Retail trade	–	–	–	336	10	326
Transportation and warehousing	156	6	150	164	14	150
Utilities	164	5	159	176	17	159
Wholesale trade	284	6	278	290	12	278
Overall	5,782	131	5,651	7,613	282	7,331

Source: Thomson Eikon data processed by the author.

and the size of the control sample is almost the same. Consistent with the relevance of concentration in spreading distress (Hertzel et al. 2008), the utilities and transportation and warehousing sectors are characterized by the highest incidence of defaulted supply relationships with respect to the total sample, from both the supplier and customer perspectives, while the

manufacturing sector presents a high incidence of defaulted supply relationships only from the supplier perspective.

For all the firms previously identified, Thomson Eikon provides data
for the full balance sheets, income statements, and financial prospectuses
from 2011 to 2016.

Methodology

By affecting interfirm relationships, an event related to the supply chain
can alter the usefulness of commercial lenders' information in predicting
business failure (Kallberg and Udell 2003) and the capability of a firm
to use trade credit to support its business by strengthening its customer
base (Summers and Wilson 2002). To test the impact of the default of
a member of the supply chain on the role of trade credit in inform-
ing and supporting growth, the analysis considers the value of account
receivables and payable around the default event, considering both the
gross and the abnormal value. In formulas, the gross value is calculated
as follows:

$$Accounts\ payable\ ratio_{it} = \frac{Accounts\ payable_{it}^{S}}{Ta_{it}^{s}} \qquad (4.1)$$

$$Accounts\ receivable\ ratio_{it} = \frac{Accounts\ receivable_{it}^{S}}{TA_{it}^{s}} \qquad (4.2)$$

where, for each firm i at time t, the ratio of accounts payable and accounts
receivable is computed considering, respectively, the amount of accounts
payable $\left(Accounts\ payable_{it}^{s}\right)$ and accounts receivable $\left(Accounts\ receivable_{it}^{s}\right)$
with respect to the total assets $\left(TA_{it}^{s}\right)$.

To consider the structural differences in trade policy in different
sectors affecting both terms and volumes (Ng, Smith, and Smith 1999),
the abnormal value is calculated based on the differences in the policy
adopted by the firm and other players in the same sector. In formulas,

$$Accounts\ payable\ ratio_{it}^{\Delta} = \frac{Accounts\ payable_{it}^{S}}{TA_{it}^{S}} - \sum_{k=1}^{n} \frac{Accounts\ payable_{kt}^{S}}{TA_{kt}^{S}}$$

$$(4.3)$$

$$Accounts\ receivable\ ratio_{it}^{\Delta} = \frac{Accounts\ receivable_{it}^{S}}{TA_{it}^{S}} - \sum_{k=1}^{n} \frac{Accounts\ receivable_{kt}^{S}}{TA_{kt}^{S}}$$

(4.4)

where the benchmark is the simple arithmetic average of values computed for all n firms included in the control sample for the same sector as the firm in question ($S = 1, ..., k$). Both groups of measures are constructed for the year before the default, the default date, and 3 years after the event.

Consistent with the literature on the usefulness of the information content of trade credit for outside investors, the analysis considers both the accounting and financial performance of the firm, proxied through the following variables (Aktas et al. 2012)[2]:

$$Z - Score_{it} = 0.012\frac{WC_{it}}{TA_{it}} + 0.014\frac{RE_{it}}{TA_{it}} + 0.333\frac{EBIT_{it}}{TA_{it}} + 0.006\frac{E_{it}}{D_{it}}$$

$$+ 0.999\frac{Sales_{it}}{TA_{it}}$$

(4.5)

$$ROA_{it} = \frac{Operating\ Income_{it}}{TA_{it}}$$

(4.6)

where, for firm i at time t,

ZScore$_{it}$ is a proxy for firm risk, computed following the approach and weights identified by Altman (1968)

$\dfrac{WC_{it}}{TA_{it}}$ is an asset structure proxy constructed as the ratio of the

working capital and total assets

$\dfrac{RE_{it}}{TA_{it}}$ is a proxy of the firm's growth opportunities, constructed as

the ratio of the amount of retained earnings and total assets

$\dfrac{EBIT_{it}}{TA_{it}}$ is a measure of profitability computed as the ratio of

earnings before interest and taxes to total assets

$\dfrac{E_{it}}{D_{it}}$ is a leverage proxy computed as the ratio of the value of equity

to the value of debt

---

[2]Jensen's alpha for the customers or suppliers of the defaulted entities is not considered, because more than 50 percent of the defaulted sample includes unlisted firms.

$\dfrac{Sales_{it}}{TA_{it}}$ is a turnover proxy constructed as the ratio of the value of
sales to total assets

ROA_{it} is a measure of the accounting performance computed as the
ratio of operating income to total assets

The analysis compares the value of the proxies constructed considering the sample of firms with defaulted customers and/or defaulted suppliers and the rest of the market considering the distance, in years, to the default event.

Having identified the differences between the performances of firms connected with defaulted firms and the others, the analysis now focuses on the implication of default on the ability of the supplier/customer of the defaulted entity to create growth. Following the approach proposed by Ferrando and Mulier (2013), the analysis extends the base model below (equation 4.7) by testing the relevance of supply chain relationships with distressed entities on value creation (equation 4.8) and whether the significance of such a variable is affected by the selection of sources to support growth, that is, bank loans versus trade credit management (equation 4.9):

$$Growth_{it}^{VA} = \alpha_0 + \alpha_1 Growth_{it-1}^{AV} + \alpha_2 TC\ Channel_{it-1} +$$
$$\alpha_3 Bank\ Loans_{it-1} + \alpha_4 Growth_{it-1}^{Sales} + \alpha_5 \ln(Size)_{it-1} +$$
$$\alpha_6 \log(Age)_{it-1} + \upsilon_i + \upsilon_t + \upsilon_{it} + \varepsilon_{it} \qquad (4.7)$$

$$Growth_{it}^{VA} = \alpha_0 + \alpha_1 Growth_{it-1}^{AV} + \alpha_2 TC\ Channel_{it-1} +$$
$$\gamma_1 Default_{it-1} + \alpha_3 Bank\ Loans_{it-1} + \alpha_4 Growth_{it-1}^{Sales} +$$
$$\alpha_5 \ln(Size)_{it-1} + \alpha_6 \log(Age)_{it-1} + \upsilon_i + \upsilon_t + \upsilon_{it} + \varepsilon_{it} \qquad (4.8)$$

$$Growth_{it}^{VA} = \alpha_0 + \alpha_1 Growth_{it-1}^{AV} + \alpha_2 TC\ Channel_{it-1} +$$
$$\gamma_2 Default_{it-1} + TC\ Channel_{it-1} + \gamma_3 Default_{it-1} \times$$
$$Bank\ Loans_{it-1} + \alpha_3 Bank\ Loans_{it-1} +$$
$$\alpha_4 Growth_{it-1}^{Sales} + \alpha_5 \ln(Size) + \alpha_6 \log(Age)_{it-1} +$$
$$\upsilon_i + \upsilon_t + \upsilon_{it} + \varepsilon_{it} \qquad (4.9)$$

where, for firm i at time t

$Growth_{it}^{VA}$ is calculated as the difference between the current and lagged values divided by the past value added. The value added is defined as the sum of profits (losses) for the period and minority interest, taxation, the cost of employees, depreciation, and interest paid.

$TC\ Channel_{it-1}$ is the trade credit channel computed as the sum of accounts receivable and accounts payable divided by total sales

$Bank\ Loans_{it-1}$ is the sum of short- and long-term financial debt scaled by total sales

$Growth_{it-1}^{Sales}$ is the growth rate of the sales value over a yearly horizon

$ln(Size)_{it-1}$ is a proxy for size computed as the natural logarithm of total assets

$log(Age)_{it-1}$ is the natural logarithm of the age

$Default_{it-1}$ is a dummy variable assuming the value of 1 if one of the relevant suppliers or customers of the firm's supply chain has already defaulted

$\upsilon_i, \upsilon_t, \upsilon_{it}$ are dummy variables for considering the fixed effect for the sector, the time, and the interaction term, respectively

All independent variables are lagged by 1 year to avoid endogeneity problems and the regression analysis is performed using a generalized method of moments panel regression model. The analysis is obtained separately for the samples of customers (defaulted and control) and suppliers (defaulted and control).

Empirical Results

The analysis of the impact of supply chain default on trade credit policy shows interesting differences with respect to average firms from the same sector (Table 4.3).

Table 4.3 Trade credit policy and supply chain default

	Supplier default			
	Account receivable/total assets		Account payable/total assets	
	Average value (%)	Δ Sector average (%)	Average value (%)	Δ Sector average (%)
−1 year	11.73	−1.85	8.81	−7.11**
Default	11.70	−1.47	8.56	−6.38**
+ 1 year	10.87	−3.09**	7.09	−8.33**
+2 years	11.80	−3.24**	9.73	−6.10**
+3 years	10.10	−5.39**	5.00	−11.83**

(continued)

Table 4.3 Trade credit policy and supply chain default (continued)

	Customer default			
	Account receivable/total assets		Account payable/total assets	
	Average value (%)	Δ Sector average (%)	Average value (%)	Δ Sector average (%)
−1 year	10.85	−2.59**	10.18	−6.82**
Default	10.74	−1.67	10.64	−5.84**
+1 year	10.25	−2.00**	11.40	−7.14**
+2 years	9.14	−1.98*	11.01	−7.65**
+3 years	9.38	−0.33	11.94	−7.52**

**Average difference statistically significant at 99% level.
*Average difference statistically significant at 95% level.
Source: Author's elaboration of Thomson Eikon data.

Firms with a defaulted supplier request, on average, significantly lower amounts of trade credit and, once the supplier defaults, the amount of accounts payable and receivable decreases immediately, as does the gap with respect to average sector increases. Consistent with the trade credit channel assumption (Ferrando and Mulier 2013), firms with defaulted suppliers are characterized by a lower ability to both obtain and offer trade credit financing opportunities. The greater reduction in obtaining trade debt is consistent with the increased insolvency risk as perceived by independent suppliers less willing to grant concessions due to the Chapter 11 filing (Wilner 2000) of the supplier's supplier and the situation not recovering over time.

If a customer defaults, the time effect on the trade receivable is not so relevant and it expires, on average, 2 years after the default. The results show that firms connected with relevant customers in default are constrained by their own suppliers in delaying payments, even before the default event. In addition, the relevance of the lack of trade debt increases once default occurs, even though it does not lead to the supplier's default before 3 years. Such results show the influence of supply chain events on interfirm financing according to a downward pattern involving suppliers' suppliers (Jorion and Zhang 2009) and potential exploitation of an abetment strategy beneficial to other rivals in supply chain interactions (Yang, Birge, and Parker 2015).

Looking at the risk and return of firms that experience defaults in their supply chain, interesting differences can be pointed out from a comparison with other firms in the same sector (Table 4.4).

Table 4.4 Supply chain default and the risk and return proxies for the linked firms

	Z-score				ROA	
	Average value	% Safe firms	% Gray zone	% Distress zone	Average value (%)	Average growth (%)
Supplier default						
− 1 year	11.08	39.62	43.40	16.98	12.22	−0.03
Default	2.32	44.00	32.00	24.00	10.79	−0.18
+ 1 year	1.20	42.86	47.62	9.52	11.28	−0.29
+2 years	2.83	30.00	60.00	10.00	12.69	−0.21
+3 years	2.89	40.00	40.00	20.00	11.85	−0.22
Customer default						
− 1 year	3.51	35.71	42.86	21.43	13.34	0.00
Default	0.51	33.02	41.51	25.47	10.43	−0.09
+ 1 year	0.38	31.25	47.92	20.83	11.60	−0.21
+2 years	2.27	31.03	51.72	17.24	13.43	−0.07
+3 years	2.53	33.03	50.00	16.67	10.96	−0.06

Source: Author's elaboration of Thomson Eikon data.

The default of relevant customers or suppliers has a significant and persistent effect on a firm's perceived default risk. On average, firms that lose a relevant supplier are those that experienced a higher and more persistent increase in credit risk, while firms that lose relevant customers need at least 2 years to obtain a comparable average risk. Regarding the classification of firms based on Z-scores, after the default of a supplier, the number of safe firms does not decrease but the number of distressed firms increases while the customer default increases the number of distress-classified firms and reduces the number of safe firms; however, after 1 year, the results tend to realign with the base scenario. In light of empirical evidence showing that riskier firms are mainly affected by idiosyncratic factors (Lopez 2004), one can conclude that the distress of connected counterparties determines the increase in insolvency risk, leading to temporary distress over the considered period.

The analysis of the average return on assets shows that default has a significant negative impact, with a decrease of more than 1.5 percent in the mean value for firms connected with defaulted suppliers and a decrease of around 3 percent for firms connected with defaulted customers. The growth rate of the return on assets registers the greatest reduction in the year of the default and the following year, the effect persisting over the period considered. Because less profitable firms are found to pay their bills later (Deloof 2003), the results for the reduction of the return on assets are consistent with the increase in insolvency risk showed by the Z-score analysis.

The last type of analysis considers the effect of supply chain default on the possibility of financing growth for the firm. The results related to customer and supplier default show interesting differences (Table 4.5).

The results (equation 4.7) are coherent with the assumption that the substitution between trade credit and bank debt is not stable over time (Huang, Shi, and Zhang 2011). The growth of the value added is normally financed using the trade credit channel and the results are confirmed for both samples analyzed (customers and suppliers), while bank credit decreases with growth development. Such evidence is consistent with the patterns for accounts receivable and payable, respectively, and bank credit after crisis events. Moreover, the trade credit channel is found to be the strongest factor affecting value creation. Consistent with the results of Martinez-Sola, Garcia-Tueruel, and Martinez-Solano (2014), a positive relation is identified for larger firms using trade credit only for entities connected with defaulted customers, while the insignificance for firms connected with defaulted suppliers can be interpreted as greater financial vulnerability in the face of a supply chain distress event (Yang 2011). A negative relation between growth and firm age (Evans 1987) is confirmed for firms connected with defaulted customers, and the high relevance of the contribution can be explained, moreover, in light of the greater complexity in restructuring the customer portfolio due to long-lasting relationships.

The default of one member of the supply chain (equation 4.8) does not affect the base model (equation 4.7) for entities connected with either defaulted suppliers or customers. The default of one member of the supply chain is found to be significant when the financing choices of growth are considered (equation 4.9). The results suggest that, upon the supply chain disruption event, firms switch from trade channel financing to bank financing. Moreover, the contribution of the interacted variable is stronger for firms connected with defaulted suppliers. The results support the hypothesis that a crisis in the supply chain network could affect the choices of sources to support the growth of the firm, leading to an increase in financial resources obtained through bank credit. Moreover, the results confirm that the relation between the use of trade credit and bank credit is not stable over time.

Table 4.5 Supply chain default and fund-raising for supporting the value-added growth

	Customers' default			Suppliers' default		
	(4.7)	**(4.8)**	**(4.9)**	**(4.7)**	**(4.8)**	**(4.9)**
$Growth_{it-1}^{VA}$	0.03**	0.01**	0.01**	−0.01	−0.01	−0.01
$TC\ Channel_{it-1}$	0.55*	0.52*	0.52*	0.75**	0.75	0.75**
$Bank\ Loans_{it-1}$	−0.09*	−0.23*	−0.23*	−0.32**	−0.32	−0.32**
$Growth_{it-1}^{Sales}$	−0,16**	−0.51*	−0.51**	0.06*	0.06	0.06*
$ln(Size)_{it-1}$	0.09**	−0.22**	0.22**	0.35	0.35	0.35
$log(Age)_{it-1}$	−0.25**	−0.45*	−0.45**	−0.05	−0.05	−0.45
$Default_{it-1}$		7.40			4.26	0.23
$Default_{it-1} \times TC\ Channel_{it-1}$			−3.36*			−7.18*
$Default_{it-1} \times Bank\ Loans_{it-1}$			3.39*			9.02*
Constant	−1.07**	3.02**	−3.13**	7.39	7.25	7.21
Firms	6,606	6,606	6,606	4,369	4,369	4,369
Industry instruments	☑	☑	☑	☑	☑	☑
Year instruments	☑	☑	☑	☑	☑	☑
Interaction instruments	☑	☑	☑	☑	☑	☑
Wald test Value and probability	69.61 (0.00)	151.86 (0.00)	151.90 (0.00)	9.56 (0.14)	9.57 (0.21)	9.57 (0.38)

Source: Author's elaboration of Thomson Eikon data.
**Statistically significant at 99% level
*Statistically significant at 95% level

Conclusions

A distinct role for trade credit has been identified as a mechanism to coordinate supply chains. Therefore, supply chain interactions can increase the information value of trade credit, as they affect the financial performance of members. The financial distress of suppliers has become a major concern for disruptions to normal activities. A supplier's financial distress is found to affect other members of the supply chain, even if the impact is influenced by counterparty exposure, the structure of the industry where supply chain interactions take place, and the type of sector.

By evaluating counterparty exposure, the results for the United States from 2012 to 2016 show that firms with defaulted suppliers are characterized by a lower ability to both obtain and offer trade credit financing opportunities. Moreover, the default of relevant customers or suppliers has a significant effect on the perceived default risk of a firm and the effect is persistent. On average, firms that lose a relevant supplier are those that experienced a greater and more persistent increase in credit risk, while firms that lose relevant customers need at least 2 years to reach a comparable average risk. Lastly, the default of one member of the supply chain does not affect the base model of the creation of value added but suggests a substitution between trade channel financing and bank financing.

Because supply chain events contribute to the information content of members' indicators, empirical evidence adds insight on both the conditions affecting the risk mitigation determined by trade receivables and the criteria to identify connected relationships between suppliers and debtors in light of the application of the standards on large exposures (see Chapter 3).

Conclusions

The risk mitigation determined by trade credit is based on credit risk. Default risk characterizes trade credit financing, as it does other financial exposures, but trade credit financing allows financiers to enlarge their information set with observations from the procurement area that are not shared with other types of financiers. Considering dilution risk, the detailed information from the procurement area allows financiers to distinguish among the different types of dilution and properly manage them to limit future losses. The complexity of risk sources in trade credit financing does not hinder the application of modern credit risk measures from producing consistent estimations of capital at risk.

The implementation of an internal rating system leads to the acknowledgment of optionality in the recognition of risk mitigation by trade credits, leaving room for both an asset and a relationship approach, depending on how the financiers manage the trade credits. The definition of default is an important and relevant issue in trade credit financing, particularly in a context with prolonged average payment terms. Therefore, proper qualifiers of the relevance of past dues with respect to total supply chain exposures should be introduced. Recovery rates are found to improve the reliability of forecasts, and the shift from assets to supply chain relationships is expected to be associated with an improvement in recovery rates. Moreover, risk mitigation is further strengthened by the short-term maturity that, at the international level, it is found to decrease. At the aggregate level, dilution risk is found to be marginal and to resolve in the short term. Nonetheless, economic sectors and contractual features matter. In light of the moderate association between concentration and credit losses, the measures implemented should address excess concentration in the origination of additional losses to preserve supply chain relationships, the source of the information advantage of trade credit financiers in the procurement area.

The application of credit risk measures to trade credit financiers is extended and can contribute significantly to value creation. The most promising application of credit risk measures is in the field of credit risk management, where the complexity of the risk management framework for trade credit financing can significantly improve pricing in light of a broader range of risks.

Capital requirements depend on the underlying credit risk of trade credits. The great flexibility of trade credits in being financed through several instruments is addressed through multiple capital treatment options. Nonetheless, the intensity of such alignment depends on the capital treatment option selected, and the current treatment of dilution risk can hamper the shift to a managerial approach intended to enhance supply chain relationships.

The economic connection linking the seller/assignor and the trade debtor is expected to be a serious issue in the risk mitigation role played by trade credits. First, it is possible to recognize that distress along the supply chain does not necessarily turn into contagion. U.S. empirical evidence shows that the effects of distress are stronger when the default of a supplier is involved, while the effects of the customer distress clear up over a shorter horizon. Second, no default chain effect is observed over the period analyzed. Lastly, because the risk of connected counterparties is perceived by financiers as increasing, the substitution effect between trade credit and bank credit prevents the further origination of high-risk trade credits, because of the control of other members of the supply chain. Such findings are relevant both from the perspective of not altering the structure of supply chain relationships by imposing inappropriate limits to finance them and in the adoption of prudential standards for large exposures. Only the analysis of supply chain relationships can help the trade credit financier qualify the accumulated trade credit over different relationships and appreciate whether the size is sufficiently excessive for its own distress and, depending on its own fundamentals, passing it to other members.

References

Agarwal, S., and F. Wang. 2009. "Perverse Incentives at the Banks? Evidence from a Natural Experiment." *Federal Reserve Bank of Chicago Working Paper*, Chicago, IL.

Allen, L., G. DeLong, and A. Saunders. 2004. "Issues in the Credit Risk Modeling of Retail Markets". *Journal of Banking and Finance* 28, no. 4, pp. 727–52.

Altman, E. 1968. "Financial Ratios. Discriminant Analysis and the Prediction of Corporate Bankruptcy". *Journal of Finance* 23, no. 4, pp. 589–609.

Altman, E. 1998. "The Importance and Subtlety of Credit Rating Migration." *Journal of Banking and Finance* 22, no. 1–2, pp. 1231–42.

Altman, E. 2002. "Managing Credit Risk: A Challenge for the New Millennium." *Economic Notes* 31, no. 2, pp. 201–214.

Altman, E., T. Baidya, and L. Ribeiro Dias. 1979. "Previsão de problemas financeiros em empresas." *Revista de Administração de Empresas* 79, no. 1, pp. 17–28.

Altman, E., and H. Izan. 1981. "Indentifying Corporate Distress in Australia. An Industry Relative Analysis." *New York University Working Paper*, New York, NY.

Altman, E., D. Kim, and Y. Eom. 1995. "Failure Prediction: Evidence from Korea." *Journal of International Financial Management and Accounting* 6, no. 3, pp. 230–59.

Altman, E., and M. Lavallee. 1981. "Business Failure Classification in Canada." *Journal of Business Administration* 12, no. 1, pp. 147–64.

Altman, E., G. Marco, and F. Varetto. 1994. Corporate Distress Diagnosis: Comparisons Using Linear Discriminant Analysis and Neural Networks (the Italian Experience). *Journal of Banking & Finance* 18, no. 3, pp. 505–29.

Altman, E., and P. Narayanan. 1997. "An International Survey of Business Failure Classification Models." *Financial Markets, Institutions and Instruments* 6, no. 2, pp. 1–97.

Altman, E., and A. Saunders. 1998. "Credit Risk Measurement: Developments Over the Last 20 Years." *Journal of Banking and Finance* 21, no. 11–12, pp. 1721–42.

Araten, M., and M. Jacobs. 2001. "Loan Equivalents for Revolving Credits and Advised Lines." *The RMA Journal* 83, no. 8, pp. 34–39.

Araten, M., J.J. Jacobs, and P. Varshney. 2004. "Measuring LGD on Commercial Loans: An 18-Year Internal Study." *RMA Journal* 86, no. 8, pp. 28–35.

Asarnow, E., and D. Edwards. 1995. "Measuring Loss on Defaulted Bank Loans: a 24-year Study." *Journal of Commercial Lending* 77, no. 7, pp. 11–23.

Asarnow, E., and E. Marker. 1995. "Historical Performance of the U.S. Corporate Loan Market: 1988-1993." *Commercial Lending Review* 10, no. 2, pp. 13–32.

Ashbaugh-Skaife, H., D. Collins, and R. LaFond. 2006. "The Effects of Corporate Governance on Firms' Credit Ratings." *Journal of Accounting and Economics* 42, no. 1–2, pp. 203–43.

Associazione Bancaria Italiana (ABI). 2002. *Loss Given Default, Aspetti metodologici e proposta di una struttura dati per la stima*. Rome, Italy: Bancaria Editrice.

Aktas, N., E. De Bodt, F. Lobez, and J. Statnik. 2012. "The Information Content of Trade Credit." *Journal of Banking and Finance* 36, no. 5, pp. 1402–13.

Babich, V., V. Burnetas, and P. Ritchken. 2007. "Competition and Diversification Effects in Supply Chains with Supplier Default Risk." *Manufacturing & Service Operations Management* 9, no. 2, pp. 123–46.

Baetge, J., M. Muss, and H. Niehaus. 1988. "The Use of Statistical Analysis to Identify the Financial Strength of Corporations in Germany." *Studies in Banking and Finance* 7, pp. 183–96.

Bai, G., and E. Elyasiani. 2013. "Bank Stability and Managerial Compensation." *Journal of Banking and Finance* 37, no. 3, pp. 799–813.

Bank of Italy. 1991. "Istruzioni relative alla classificazione della clientela per settori e gruppi di attivita' economica." *Circolare,* no. 140.

Bank of Italy. 2001. "Questionario sul recupero crediti: principali risultati." *Bollettino di vigilanza,* no. 12, Rome, Italy.

Barber, B., R. Lehavy, and B. Trueman. 2007. "Comparing the Stock Recommendation Performance of Investment Banks and Independent Research Firms." *Journal of Financial Economics* 85, no. 2, pp. 490–517.

Basel Committee on Banking Supervision. 1999. *Credit Risk Modelling: Current Practices and Applications*. Basel, Switzerland.

Basel Committee on Banking Supervision. 2000. *Principles for the Management of Credit Risk*. Basel, Switzerland.

Basel Committee on Banking Supervision. 2004. *International Convergence of Capital Measurement and Capital Standards*. Basel, Switzerland.

Basel Committee on Banking Supervision. 2005a. *Guidance on Paragraph 468 of the Framework Document*. Basel, Switzerland.

Basel Committee on Banking Supervision. 2005b. "Studies on the Validation of Internal Rating Systems." *Working Paper,* no. 14, Basel, Switzerland.

Basel Committee on Banking Supervision. 2006. *International Convergence of Capital Measurement and Capital Standards: A Revised Framework*. Basel, Switzerland.

Basel Committee on Banking Supervision. 2014. *Supervisory Framework for Measuring and Controlling Large Exposures*. Basel, Switzerland.

Basel Committee on Banking Supervision. 2017a. *Thirteenth Progress Report on Adoption of the Basel Regulatory Framework.* Basel, Switzerland.

Basel Committee on Banking Supervision. 2017b. *Capital Treatment for Simple, Transparent and Comparable Short-term Securitisations.* Consultative document, Basel, Switzerland.

Bhatia, U. 1988. "Predicting Corporate Sickness in India." *Studies in Banking and Finance* 7, pp. 57–71.

Berg, T., M. Puri, and J. Rocholl. 2013. "Loan Officer Incentives and the Limits of Hard Information." *NBER Working Paper* no. 19051, Cambridge, MA.

Berger, A., and G. Udell. 1995. "Relationship Lending and Line of Credit in Small Firm Finance." *Journal of Business* 68, no. 3, pp. 351–81.

Bessis, J. 2015. *Risk Management in Banking.* Hoboken, NJ: Wiley.

Bielecki, T., S. Crepey, and M. Jeanblanc. 2010. "Up and Down Credit Risk." *Journal of Quantitative Finance* 10, no. 10, pp. 1137–51.

Bilderbeek, J. 1979. "An Empirical Study of the Predictive Ability of Financial Ratios in the Netherlands." *Zeitschrift fr Betriebswirtschaft*, no. 5, pp. 388–407.

Boissay, F., and R. Gropp. 2013. "Payment Defaults and Interfirm Liquidity Provision." *Review of Finance* 17, no. 6, pp. 1853–94.

Bonini, S., and G. Caivano. 2013. "The Survival Analysis Approach in Basel II Credit Risk Management: Modeling Danger Rates in the Loss Given Default Parameter." *Journal of Credit Risk* 9, no. 1, pp. 101–18.

Boot, A., T. Milbourn, and A. Schmeits. 2006. "Credit Ratings as Coordination Mechanisms." *Review of Financial Studies* 19, no. 1, pp. 81–118.

Brady, B., P. Chang, P. Miu, B. Ozdemir, and D. Schwartz. 2006. "Discount Rate for Workout Recoveries: an Empirical Study," *SSRN Electronic Journal.* http://dx.doi.org/10.2139/ssrn.907073

Brunner, A., J. Krahnen, and M. Weber. 2000. "Information Production in Credit Relationships on the Role of Internal Ratings in Commercial Banking." *Working Papers, Center of Financial Studies*, no. 10, Frankfurt, Germany.

Cantor, R., and F. Packer. 1996. "Determinants and Impact of Sovereign Credit Ratings." *Economic Policy Review* 2, no. 2, pp. 37–53.

Capeci, J. 1991. "Credit Risk, Credit Ratings, and Municipal Bond Yields: A Panel Study." *National Tax Journal* 44, no. 4, pp. 41–56.

Capon, N. 1982. "Credit Scoring Systems: A Critical Analysis." *Journal of Marketing* 46, no. 2, pp. 82–91.

Carbo Valverde, S., F. Rodriguez-Fernandez, and G. Udell. 2016. "Trade Credit, the Financial Crises and SME Access to Finance." *Journal of Money, Credit and Banking* 48, no. 1, pp. 113–43.

Carey, M., and M. Gordy. 2004. "Measuring Systematic Risk in Recoveries on Defaulted Debt I: Firm-level Ultimate LGDs." *FDIC Center for Financial Research Working Paper*, Washington, DC.

Carey, M., and M. Hrycay. 2001. "Parameterizing Credit Risk Models with Rating Data." *Journal of Banking and Finance* 25, no. 1, pp. 197–270.

Carty, L., D. Hamilton, and A. Moss. 1999. "Bankrupt Bank Loan Recoveries." *Journal of Lending and Credit Risk Management* 81, no. 10, pp. 20–26.

Caselli, S., and S. Gatti. 2003. *Il Corporate Lending*. Rome, Italy: Bancaria Editrice.

Christian, P. 2006. "Estimating Loss Given Default –Experiences from Banking Practice." In *The Basel II Risk Parameters – Estimation, Validation and Stress Testing*, eds. B. Engelmann, and R. Rauhmeier. Heidelberg, Germany: Springer.

Coleman, A., N. Esho, and I. Sharpe. 2006. "Does Bank Monitoring Influence Loan Contract Terms?" *Journal of Financial Services Research* 30, no. 2, pp. 177–98.

Couwenberg, O., and A. De Jong. 2008. "Costs and Recovery Rates in the Dutch Liquidation-based Bankruptcy System." *European Journal of Law Economics* 26, no. 2, pp. 105–27.

Covitz, D., and S. Han. 2004. "An Empirical Analysis of Bond Recovery Rates: Exploring the Structural View of Default." *Federal Reserve Board Working Paper*, Washington, DC.

Cowan, A., and C. Cowan. 2004. "Default Correlation: An Empirical Investigation of a Subprime Lender." *Journal of Banking and Finance* 28, no. 4, pp. 753–71.

Crook, R., and J. Combs. 2007. "Sources and Consequences of Bargaining Power in Supply Chains." *Journal of Operations Management* 25, no. 2, pp. 546–55.

Crouhy, M., D. Galai, and R. Mark. 2000. "A Comparative Analysis of Current Credit Risk Models." *Journal of Banking and Finance* 24, no. 1–2, pp. 59–117.

Crouhy, M., D. Galai, and R. Mark. 2001. "Prototype Risk Rating System." *Journal of Banking and Finance* 25, no. 1, pp. 47–95.

D'Avanzo, R., H. Lewinski, and L. Van Wassenhove. 2003. "The Link Between Supply Chain and Financial Performance." *Supply Chain Management Review* 7, no. 6, pp. 40–47.

Danielsson, J., Jorgensen B. and de Vreis C. (2002). "Incentives for effective risk management." *Journal of Banking and Finance* 26, no. 7, pp.1407-1425.

Davydenko, A., and J. Franks. 2008. "Do Bankruptcy Codes Matter? A Study of Defaults in France, Germany, and the UK." *Journal of Finance* 63, no. 2, pp. 565–608.

De Laurentis, G. 2001. *Rating interni e credit risk management*. Rome, Italy: Bancaria Editrice.

De Laurentis, G., R. Maino, and L. Molteni. 2010. *Developing, Validating and Using Internal Ratings, Methodologies and Case Studies*. Hoboken, NJ: John Wiley and Sons.

De Laurentis, G., and M. Riani. 2005. "Estimating LGD in the Leasing Industry: Empirical Evidence from a Multivariate Model." In *Recovery Risk: The Next Challenge in Credit Risk Management,* eds. E. Altman, A. Resti, and A. Sironi. London, UK: Risk Books.

De Leonardis, D., and R. Rocci. 2014. "Default Risk Analysis via a Discrete-time Cure Rate Model." *Applied Stochastic Models in Business and Industry* 30, no. 5, pp. 529–43.

Del Prete, S., M. Pagnini, P. Rossi, and V. Vacca. 2014. "Lending Organization in Italian Banks." *Bancaria* 1, pp. 62–80.

Del Prete, S., M. Pagnini, P. Rossi, and V. Vacca. 2017. "Lending Organization and Credit Supply During the 2008-09 Crisis." *Bank of Italy Working Paper* no. 1108, Rome, Italy.

Deloof, M. 2003. "Does Working Capital Management Affect Profitability of Belgian Firms?" *Journal of Business and Financial Accounting* 30, no. 3–4, pp. 573–88.

Dermine, J., and C. Neto de Carvalho. 2006. "Bank Loan Loss Given Default: A Case Study." *Journal of Banking and Finance* 30, no. 4, pp. 1219–43.

Dietch, M., and J. Petey. 2004. "Should SME Exposures Be Treated as Retail or Corporate Exposures? A Comparative Analysis of Default Probabilities and Asset Correlations in French and German SMEs." *Journal of Banking and Finance* 28, no. 4, pp. 773–88.

Dionne, G., and T. Harchaoui. 2008. "Bank Capital, Securitization and Credit Risk: An Empirical Evidence." *Insurance and Risk Management* 75, no. 4, pp. 459–85.

Dorfleitner, G., J. Rad, and M. Weber. 2017. "Pricing in the Online Invoice Trading Market: First Empirical Evidence." *Economic Letters* 161, pp. 56–61.

Dyckman, B. 2011. "Supply Chain Finance: Risk Mitigation and Revenue Growth." *Journal of Corporate Treasury Management* 4, no. 2, pp. 168–73.

Earl, M., and D. Marais. 1982. "Predicting Corporate Failure in the U.K. Using Discriminant Analysis." *Accounting and Business Research*.

Ellinger, A., M. Natarajarathinam, F. Adams, J.B. Gray, D. Hofman, and K. O'Marah. 2011. "Supply Chain Management Competency and Firm Financial Success." *Journal of Business Logistics* 32, no. 3, pp. 214–26.

European Banking Authority. 2016. *Guidelines on the Application of the Definition of Default Under Article 178 of Regulation (EU),* no. 575/2013, Final Report, London, UK.

European Commission. 2015. "Regulation (EU) 2015/227." *Official Journal of the European Union,* L.48/1.

European Parliament and Council. 2006. "Directive 2006/49/EC of 14 June 2006 on the Capital Adequacy of Investment Firms and Credit Institutions (Recast)." *Official Journal of the European Union,* L.177/201.

Evans, D. 1987. "The Relationship Between Firm Growth, Size and Age: Estimates for 100 Manufacturing Industries." *Journal of Industrial economics* 35, no. 4, pp. 567–81.

Fernandez, A. 1988. "A Spanish Model for Credit Risk Classification." *Studies in Banking and Finance* 7, pp. 115–25.

Ferrando, A. and Mulier, K. (2013). "Do firms use the trade credit channel to manage growth?". *Journal of Banking and Finance* 37, no.8, pp.3035-3046.

Fisman, R., and I. Love. 2003. "Trade Credit, Financial Intermediary Development, and Industry Growth." *Journal of Finance* 58, no. 1, pp. 353–74.

Foglia, A., S. Iannotti, and P. Marullo Reedtz. 2001. "The Definition of the Grading Scales in Banks' Internal Rating Systems." *Economic Notes* 30, no. 3, pp. 421–56.

Froot, K., and J. Stein. 1998. "Risk Management, Capital Budgeting, and Capital Structure Policy for Financial Institutions: An Integrated Approach." *Journal of Financial Economics* 47, no. 1, pp. 55–82.

Frye, J. 2000. "Collateral Damage: A Source of Systematic Credit Risk." *Risk Magazine* 13, no. 4, pp. 28–29.

Funatsu, H. 1986. "Export Credit Insurance." *Journal of Risk and Insurance* 53, no. 4, pp. 679–92.

Garcia-Appendini, E., and J. Montoriol-Garriga. 2015. "Trade Credit Use as Firms Approach Default." University of St. Gallen, School of Finance Research Paper, no. 11.

Giannotti, C., and L. Gibilaro. 2009. "Property Market Liquidity and Real Estate Recovery Procedures: Evidences from the Italian Economic Cycle." *Journal of European Real Estate Research* 2, no. 3, pp. 235–58.

Gibilaro, L. 2006a. "I fabbisogni informativi del processo di rating interno per il portafoglio corporate delle banche: il caso della Loss Given Default." In *Informazione e governo del rischio di credito*, eds. A. Carretta, U. Filotto, and F. Fiordelisi. Rome, Italy: Franco Angeli.

Gibilaro, L. 2006b. "L'impatto del Nuovo Accordo sul Capitale sulla standardizzazione dei processi del risk management: il rischio di dilution", *I processi di standardizzazione in azienda, Aspetti istituzionali, organizzativi, manageriali, finanziari e contabili, Atti del X Convegno nazionale di Aidea Giovani Dipartimento di Studi Aziendali Università degli studi di Napoli Parthenope 17-18 marzo 2005*, ed. AA.VV. Rome, Italy: Franco Angeli.

Gibilaro, L., and G. Mattarocci. 2007. "The Selection of the Discount Rate in Estimating Loss Given Default." *Global Journal of Business Research* 1, no. 1, pp. 15–33.

Gibilaro, L., and G. Mattarocci. 2009. "Concentration in Lending: Commercial vs Financial Credits." *Academy of Banking Studies Journal* 8, no. 1, pp. 39–60.

Gibilaro, L., and G. Mattarocci. 2011. "The impact of Discount Rate Choice in Estimating the Workout LGD." *Journal of Applied Business Research* 27, no. 2, pp. 139–48.

Gibilaro, L., and G. Mattarocci. 2012. "The Impact of Discount Rate Choice in Estimating the Workout LGD for Corporate and Retail Portfolios." In *Financial Systems in Troubled Waters Information, Strategies, and Governance to Enhance Performances in Risky Times.* eds. A. Carretta, and G. Mattarocci. Abingdon, UK: Routledge.

Gini, C. 1936. "On the Measure of Concentration with Special Reference to Income and Wealth." In *Abstracts of papers presented at the Cowles Commission Research Conference on Economics and Statistics.* Colorado Springs, CO: Colorado College Press.

Gloubos, G., and T. Grammatikos. 1988. "The Success of Bankruptcy Prediction Models in Greece." *Studies in Banking and Finance* 7, pp. 37–46.

Gordy, M.B. 2003. "A Risk Factor Model Foundation for Ratings-based Bank Capital Rules." *Journal of Financial Intermediation* 12, no. 3, pp. 199–232.

Gordy, M.B., and E. Luetkebohmert. 2013. "Granularity Adjustments for Regulatory Capital Assessment." *International Journal of Central Banking* 9, no. 3, pp. 38–77.

Group of Thirty. 2013. "A New Paradigm: Financial Institution Boards and Supervisors." Special Report, Washington, DC: Group of Thirty.

Grunert, J., L. Norden, and M. Weber. 2004. "The Role of Non-financial Factors in Internal Credit Ratings." *Journal of Banking and Finance* 29, no. 2, pp. 509–31.

Grunert, J., and M. Weber. 2009. "Recovery Rates of Commercial Lending: Empirical Evidence for German Companies." *Journal of Banking and Finance* 33, no. 3, pp. 505–13.

Gupton, G. 2005. "Advancing Loss Given Default Prediction Models: How the Quiet have Quickened." *Economic Notes* 34, no. 2, pp. 185–230.

Hackbarth, D., J. Miao, and E. Morellec. 2006. "Capital Structure, Credit Risk, and Macroeconomic Conditions." *Journal of Finance Economics* 82, no. 3, pp. 519–50.

Hallikas, J., K. Puumalainen, T. Vesterinen, and V.M. Viroleinen. 2005. "Risk-based Classification of Supplier Relationships." *Journal of Purchasing and Supply Management* 11, no. 11–12, pp. 72–82.

Hàjek, P. 2011. "Municipal Credit Rating Modelling by Neural Networks." *Decision Support Systems* 51, no. 2, pp. 108–18.

Hamilton, D.T., and L.V. Carthy. 1999. "Debt recoveries for corporate bankruptcies", *Special Comment, Moody's Investors Service,* June, New York.

Hart, P.E. 1971. "Entropy and Other Measures of Concentration." *Journal of the Royal Statistic Society Series A* 134, no. 1, pp. 73–85.

Hartmann-Wendels, T., P. Miller, and E. Toews. 2014. "Loss Given Default for Leasing: Parametric and Nonparametric Estimations." *Journal of Banking and Finance* 40, no. 1, pp. 364–75.

Heider, F., and R. Inderst. 2012. "Loan Prospecting." *Review of Financial Studies* 25, no. 8, pp. 2381–415.

Heitfield, E., Burton, S. and Chomsisengphet, S. (2005). "Risk Sensitive Regulatory Capital Rules for Hedged Credit Exposures". In *Counterparty Credit Risk Modelling: Pricing, Risk Management and Regulation*, ed. Pykhtin, M. London: Risk Waters Group.

Hendricks, K., and V. Singhal. 2003. "The Effect of Supply Chain Glitches on Shareholder Value." *Journal of Operations Management* 21, no. 5, pp. 501–22.

Hendricks, K.B., and V.R. Singhal. 2005. "An Empirical Analysis of the Effect of Supply Chain Disruptions on Long-run Stock Price Performance and Risk of the Firm." *Production and Operations Management* 14, no. 1, pp. 35–52.

Hertzel, M.G., Z. Li, M. Officer, and K. Rodgers. 2008. "Inter-firm Linkages and the Wealth Effects of Financial Distress Along the Supply Chain." *Journal of Financial Economics* 87, no. 2, pp. 374–87.

Hlawatsch, S., and S. Ostrowski. 2011. "Simulation and Estimation of Loss Given Default." *Journal of Credit Risk* 7, no. 3, pp. 39–73.

Hofman, E., and O. Belin. 2011. "Characteristics of SCF." In *Supply Chain Finance Solutions, SpringerBriefs in Business,* eds. E. Hofman, and O. Belin. Heidelberg, Germany: Springer.

Huang, H., X. Shi, and S. Zhang. 2011. "Counter-cyclical Substitution Between Trade Credit and Bank Credit." *Journal of Banking and Finance* 35, no. 8, pp. 1859–78.

IFRS Foundation. 2005. *IFRS 9 Financial Instruments*, London, UK.

Izan, H. 1984. "Corporate Distress in Australia." *Journal of Banking and Finance* 8, no. 2, pp. 303–20.

Izvorski, I. 1997. "Recovery Ratios and Survival Times for Corporate Bonds." *International Monetary Fund Working Paper*, no. 9784, Washington, DC.

Jimenez, G., J.A. Lopez, and J. Saurina. 2009. "Empirical Analysis of Corporate Credit Lines." *Review of Financial Studies* 22, no. 12, pp. 5069–98.

Jones, S. and Walker, R. 2007. "Explanators of Local Government Distress", *Abacus* 43, no. 3, pp. 396–418.

Jones, P. 2010. "Trade Credit Insurance." *Primer Series on Insurance*, no. 15.

Jorion, P. 2007. *Value at Risk: The New Benchmark for Managing Financial Risk.* New York, NY: McGraw Hill.

Jorion, P., and G. Zhang. 2009. "Credit Contagion from Counterparty Risk." *Journal of Finance*, 64, no. 5, pp. 2053–87.

Kallberg, J.G., and G. Udell. 2003. "The Value of Private Sector Business Credit Information Sharing: The US Case." *Journal of Banking and Finance* 27, no. 3, pp. 449–69.

Katz, A. 2011. "Accounts Receivables Securitization." *Journal of Structured Finance* 17, no. 2, pp. 23–27.

Kiff, J., F. Michaud, and J. Mitchell. 2003. "An Analytical Review of Credit Risk Transfer Instruments." *Financial Stability Review* 1, no. 1, pp. 125–50.

Kirschermann, K., and L. Norden. 2012. "The Relationship Between Borrower Risk and Loan Maturity in Small Business Lending." *Journal of Business Finance and Accounting* 39, no. 5–6, pp. 730–57.

Kiyotaki, N., and Moore, J. 1997. *Credit chains*, mimeo.

Kleindorfer, P., and G. Saad. 2005. "Managing Disruption Risks in Supply Chains." *Production and Operations Management* 14, no. 1, pp. 53–56.

Ko, C. 1982. "A Delineation of Corporate Appraisal Models and Classification of Bankruptcy Firms in Japan." *New York University Working Paper*, New York, NY.

Lajili, K., and D. Zeghal. 2005. "A Content Analysis of Risk Management Disclosures in Canadian Annual Reports." *Canadian Journal of Administrative Sciences* 22, no. 2, pp. 125–42.

Lambert, D., M. Cooper, and J. Pagh. 1998. "Supply Chain Management: Implementation Issues and Research Opportunities." *International Journal of Logistic Management* 9, no. 2, pp. 1–19.

Lang, L., and R. Stulz. 1992. "Contagion and Competitive Intra-industry Effects of Bankruptcy Announcements." *Journal of Financial Economics* 32, no. 1, pp. 45–66.

Lewellen, W.G., J.J. McConnel, and J.A. Scott. 1980. "Capital Market Influence on Trade Credit Policy." *Journal of Financial Research* 3, no. 1, pp. 105–13.

Lin, S., J. Ansell, and J. Adreeva. 2012. "Predicting Default of a Small Business Using Different Definitions of Financial Distress." *Journal of the Operational Research Society* 63, no. 4, pp. 539–48.

Linsey, P., and P. Shrives. 2006. "Risk Reporting: A Study of Risk Disclosures in the Annual Reports of UK Companies." *British Accounting Review* 38, no. 4, pp. 387–404.

Livne, G., G. Markarian, and M. Mironov. 2013. "Investment Horizon, Risk, and Compensation in the Banking Industry." *Journal of Banking and Finance* 37, no. 9, pp. 3669–80.

Ljungqvist, A., F. Marston, L. Starks, K. Wei, and H. Yan. 2007. "Conflicts of Interest in Sell-side Research and the Moderating Role of Institutional Investors." *Journal of Financial Economics* 85, no. 2, p. 420–56.

Longhofer, S.D., and J.A. Santos. 2003. "The Paradox of Priority." *Financial Management* 32, no. 1, pp. 69–81.

Lopez, J.A. 2004. "The Empirical Relationship Between Average Asset Correlation, Firm Probability of Default, and Asset Size." *Journal of Financial Intermediation* 13, no. 2, pp. 265–83.

Lucas, D. 1995. "Default Correlation and Credit Analysis." *Journal of Fixed Income* 4, no. 4, pp. 76–87.

Luo, J., and Q. Zhang. 2012. "Trade Credit: A New Mechanism to Coordinate Supply Chain." *Operations Research Letters* 40, no. 5, pp. 378–84.

Marais, D. 1979. "A Method of Quantifying Companies' Relative Financial Strength." *Bank of England Working Paper* 4, London, UK.

Martinez-Sola, C., P. Garcia-Tueruel, and P. Martinez-Solano. 2014. "Trade Credit and SME Profitability." *Small Business Economics* 42, no. 3, pp. 561–77.

Mehran, H., and R. Stulz. 2007. "The Economics of Conflicts of Interest in Financial Institutions." *Journal of Financial Economics* 85, no. 2, pp. 267–97.

Meltzer, A.H. 1960. "Mercantile Credit, Monetary Policy, and Size of Firms." *Review of Economics and Statistics* 42, no. 4, pp. 429–37.

Merton, R. 1974. "On the Pricing of Corporate Debt: The Risk Structure of Interest Rates." *Journal of Finance* 29, no. 2, pp. 449–70.

Mian, S.L., and C.W. Smith. 1992. "Accounts Receivable Management Policy: Theory and Evidence." *Journal of Finance* 47, no. 1, pp. 169–200.

Mester, L., L. Nakamura, and M. Renault. 2007. "Transactions Accounts and Loan Monitoring." *Review of Financial Studies* 20, no. 3, pp. 529–56.

Ng, C.K., J.K. Smith, and R.L. Smith. 1999. "Evidence on the Determinants of Credit Terms Used in Interfirm Trade." *Journal of Finance* 54, no. 3, pp. 1109–29.

Nocco, B., and R. Stulz. 2006. "Enterprise Risk Management: Theory and Practice." *Journal of Applied Corporate Finance* 18, no. 4, pp. 8–20.

Norden, L., and M. Szerencses. 2006. "Migration and Concentration Risk in Bank Lending: New Evidence from Credit Portfolio Data." *University of Mannheim Working Paper*, Mannheim, Germany.

Palia, D., and J. Sopranzetti. 2004. "Securitizing Accounts Receivable." *Review of Quantitative Finance and Accounting* 22, no. 1, pp. 29–38.

Pascale, R. 1988. "A Multivariate Model to Predict Firm Financial Problems: The Case of Uruguay." *Studies in Banking and Finance* 7, pp. 171–82.

Peter, C. 2006. "Estimating Loss Given Default, Experiences from banking practice." In *The Basel II Risk Parameters, Estimation, Validation, and Stress Testing*, eds. B. Engelmann, and R. Rauhmeier. Heidelberg, Germany: Springer.

Petersen, M., and R. Rajan. 1997. "Trade Credit: Theories and Evidence." *Review of Financial Studies* 10, no. 3, pp. 661–91.

Piersante, F. 2012. *Past due: fu vero default?*, mimeo.

Pu, L., and A. Thakor. 1984. "Interest Yields, Credit Ratings, and Economic Characteristics of State Bonds: An Empirical Analysis." *Journal of Money, Credit and Banking* 16, no. 3, pp. 344–51.

Querci, F. 2007. *Rischio di credito e valutazione della Loss Given Default*. Rome, Italy: Bancaria Editrice.

Qi, M., and X. Zhao. 2011. "Comparison of Modeling Methods for Loss Given Default." *Journal of Banking and Finance* 35, no. 11, pp. 2842–55.

Qian, J., P. Strahan, and Z. Yang. 2015. "The Impact of Incentives and Communication Costs on Information Production and Use: Evidence from Bank Lending." *Journal of Finance* 70, no. 4, pp. 1457–93.

Raddatz, C. 2010. "Credit Chains and Sectoral Comovement: Does the Use of Trade Credit Amplify Sectoral Shocks?" *Review of Economics and Statistics* 92, no. 4, pp. 985–1003.

Repullo, R., and J. Suarez. 2004. "Loan Pricing Under Basel Capital Requirements." *Journal of Financial Intermediation* 13, no. 4, pp. 496–521.

Resti, A., and A. Sironi. 2007a. "Defining LGD: the Basel II Perspective." In *Recovery Risk: The Next Challenge in Credit Risk Management*, eds. E. Altman, A. Resti, and A. Sironi. London, UK: Risk Books.

Resti, A., and A. Sironi. 2007b. *Risk Management and Shareholders' Value in Banking: From Risk Measurement Models to Capital Allocation Policies*. Hoboken, NJ: Wiley and Sons.

Reuter, L. 2006. "Loan Administration for Asset-Based Loans." *RMA Journal*, pp. 30–33.

Riestra, A. 2003. "Credit Insurance in Europe, Impact, Measurement and Policy Recommendations." *CEPS Research Report in Finance and Banking*, no. 31, Brussels, Belgium.

Rikkers, F., and A. Thibeault. 2007. "The Optimal Rating Philosophy for the Rating of the SME." *Vlerick Leuven Gent Working Paper*, no. 10, University of Leuven, Belgium.

Ruozi, R., and B. Rossignoli. 1985. *Manuale del factoring*. Milano, Italy: Giuffrè.

Saita, F. 1999. "Allocation of Risk Capital in Financial Institutions." *Financial Management* 28, no. 3, pp. 95–111.

Saita, F. 2004. "Il controllo dei rating assegnati." In *Rating interni e controllo del rischio di credito*, eds. G. De Laurentis, F. Saita, and A. Sironi. Rome, Italy: Bancaria editrice.

Salas, V., and J. Saurina. 2002. "Credit Risk in Two Institutional Regimes: Spanish Commercial and Savings Banks." *Journal of Financial Services Research* 22, no. 3, pp. 203–24.

Schockley, R., and A. Thakor. 1997. "Bank Loan Commitments Contracts: Data Theory and Tests." *Journal of Money, Credit, and Banking* 29, no. 4, pp. 517–34.

Schuermann, T. 2004. "What Do We Know About Loss Given Default?" In *Credit Risk Models and Management*, ed. D. Schimko. London, UK: Risk Books.

Shannon, C.E. 1948. "A Mathematical Theory of Communication." *Bell System Technical Journal* 27, no. 3, pp. 379–423.

Sokolovska, O. 2017. "Trade Credit Insurance and Information Asymmetric Information Problem." *Scientific Annals of Economics and Business* 64, no. 1, pp. 123–37.

Sopranzetti, B.J. 1998. "The Economics of Factoring Accounts Receivable." *Journal of Economics and Business* 50, no. 4, pp. 339–59.

Spuchľáková, E., K. Valaškováb, and P. Adamko. 2015. "The Credit Risk and Its Measurement, Hedging and Monitoring." *Procedia Economics and Finance* 24, pp. 675–85.

Standard & Poor's. 2004. *U.S. Trade Receivable Securitization: Offset Risk under Long-Term Contracts*, January.

Stevens, G.C. 1989. "Integrating the Supply Chain." *International Journal of Physical Distribution & Materials Management* 19, no. 8, pp. 3–8.

Stulz, R. 2008. "Risk Management Failures: What Are They and When Do They Happen?" *Journal of Applied Corporate Finance* 20, no. 4, pp. 39–48.

Summer, B. and Wilson, N. (2002). "An empirical investigation of trade credit demand". *International Journal of the Economics and Business* 9, no. 2, pp. 257–270.

Suominen, S. 1988. "The Prediction of Bankruptcy in Finland." *Studies in Banking and Finance* 7, pp. 27–36.

Ta, H., and L. Seah. 1988. "Business Failure Prediction in Singapore." *Studies in Banking and Finance* 7, pp. 105–13.

Taffler, R. 1982. "Forecasting Company Failure in the U.K. Using Discriminant Analysis and Financial Ratios Data." *Journal of Royal Statistical Society* 145, no. 3, pp. 342–58.

Taffler, R., and H. Tisshaw. 1977. "Going, Going Going: Four Factors Which Predict." *Accountancy* 88, no. 1003, pp. 50–54.

Takahashi, K., Y. Kurokawa, and K. Watase. 1979. "Financial Characteristics of Bankrupt Firms." *Keio Management*, April, pp. 40–64.

Tasche, D. 2008. "Validation of Internal Rating Systems and PD Estimates." In *Quantitative Finance: The Analytics of Risk Model Validation*, eds. G. Christodoulakis, and S. Satchell. Cambridge, MA: Academic Press.

Terradez, M., R. Kizys, A. Juan, A. Debon, and B. Sawik. 2015. "Risk Scoring Models for Trade Credit in Small and Medium Enterprises." In *Theory and Practice of Risk Assessment*, eds. C. Kitsos, T. Oliveira, A. Rigas, and S. Gulati. Springer Proceedings in Mathematics & Statistics, vol. 136. Cham, Switzerland: Springer International Publishing.

Titman, S., and R. Wessels. 1988. "The Determinants of Capital Structure." *Journal of Finance* 43, no. 1, pp. 1–40.

Tong, E., C. Mues, and L. Thomas. 2012. "Mixture Cure Models in Credit Scoring: If and When Borrowers Default." *European Journal of Operational Research* 218, no. 1, pp. 132–39.

Träuck, S., S. Harpainter, and S.T. Rachev. 2005. "A Note on Forecasting Aggregate Recovery Rates with Macroeconomic Variables." *University of Karlsruhe Working Paper*, Karlsruhe, Germany.

Treacy, W. and Carey M. 1998. "Credit risk rating at large U.S. banks". *Federal Reserve Bulletin,*no.84, pp. 897–921.

Treacy, W., and M. Carey. 2000. "Credit Risk Rating Systems at Large US Banks." *Journal of Banking and Finance* 24, no. 1–2, pp. 167–201.

Tschemernjak, R. 2004. "Assessing the Regulatory Impact: Credit Risk – Going Beyond Basel II." *Balance Sheet* 12, no. 4, pp. 37–41.

Ughetto, E. 2008. "The Financing of Innovative Activities of Banking Institutions: Policy Issues and Regulatory Options." In *Powerful Finance and Innovation Trends in a High Risk Economy,* eds. B. Laperche, D. Uzunidis. Basingstoke, UK: Palgrave Macmillan.

Unal, T. 1988. "An Early Warning Model of Predicting Firm Failure in Turkey." *Studies in Banking and Finance* 7, 141–70.

Van de Castle, K., and D. Keisman. 2000. "Suddenly Structure Mattered: Insights into Recoveries of Defaulted." *S&P Corporate Ratings,* May.

Van der Veer, K.J.M. 2015. "The Private Export Credit Insurance Effect on Trade." *Journal of Risk and Insurance* 82, no. 3, pp. 601–23.

Van Horen, N. 2007. "Customer Market Power and the Provision of Trade Credit, Evidence from Eastern Europe and Central Asia." *Policy Research Working Paper,* no. 4284, World Bank, Washington, DC.

Vasicek, O. 2002. "Loan Portfolio Value." *Risk,* December.

Von Stein, J., and W. Ziegler. 1984. "The Prognosis and Surveillance of Risks from Commercial Credit Borrowers." *Journal of Banking and Finance* 8, no. 2, pp. 249–68.

Wagner, S., and C. Bode. 2006. "An Empirical Investigation into Supply Chain Vulnerability." *Journal of Purchasing and Supply Management* 12, no. 6, pp. 301–12.

Wagner, S., C. Bode, and P. Koziol. 2008. "Supplier Default Dependencies: Empirical Evidence from the Automotive Industry." *European Journal of Operational Research* 199, no. 1, pp. 150–61.

Wagner, S., and C. Bode. 2011. "A Credit Risk Modelling Approach to Assess Supplier Default Risk." In *Operations Research Proceedings 2010, Operations Research Proceedings (GOR (Gesellschaft für Operations Research e.V.),* eds. B. Hu, K. Morasch, S. Pickl, and M. Siegle. Heidelberg, Germany: Springer.

Weibel, P. 1973. *The Value of Criteria to Judge Credit Worthiness in the Lending of Banks.* Berne/Stuttgart: Wharton Financial Institutions Centre.

Wilner, B. 2000. "The Exploitation of Relationships in Financial Distress: The Case of Trade Credit." *Journal of Finance* 55, no. 1, pp. 153–78.

Yang, X. 2011. "The Role of Trade Credit in the Recent Subprime Financial Crisis." *Journal of Economics and Business* 63, no. 5, pp. 517–29.

Yang, A., J. Birge, and R. Parker. 2015. "The Supply Chain Effects of Bankruptcy." *Management Science* 61, no. 10, pp. 2320–38.

Yu, M. 2013. "Supply Chain Management and Financial Performance: Literature Review and Future Directions." *International Journal of Production Economics* 33, no. 10, pp. 1283–317.

Zaik, E., J. Walter, G. Retting, and C. James. 1996. "RAROC at Bank of America: From Theory to Practice." *Journal of Applied Corporate Finance* 9, no. 2, pp. 83–93.

Zaniboni, N.C., A.C. De Araùjo, and A. De Avila Montini. 2013. "Factors that influence LGD for Retail Loans in Financial Institutions." *Sixth Brazilian Conference on Statistical Modelling in Insurance and Finance*, São Paulo, Brazil, pp. 2–13.

Zhang. S., and Q. Li. 2010. "A Review of Supply Chain Risk Management: From the Perspective of Default Correlation." *2010 International Conference on Management of e-Commerce and e-Government*, IEEE Computer Society, Los Alamitos, CA.

Zhang, B., P. Baeck, T. Ziegler, J. Bone, and K. Garvey. 2016. *Pushing Boundaries, The 2015 UK Alternative Finance Industry Report*, Nesta and Cambridge Center for Alternative Finance.

Zhao, J.Y., D.W. Dwyer, and J. Zhang. 2014. "Usage and Exposures at Default of Corporate Credit Lines: an Empirical Study." *Journal of Credit Risk* 10, no. 1, pp. 65–86.

Online Sources

Association Française des Sociétes Financières (ASF) (2003). *Position of the ASF on the Third Consultative Paper of the Basel Committee.* https://www.bis.org/bcbs/cp3/asfrdesofi.pdf, (May 20, 2015 accessed)

Associazione Italiana Financial Industry Risk Managers (AIFIRM) (2016), "Validation of rating models calibration", *position paper*, https://www.finriskalert.it/?p=3590, (December 1, 2018 accessed)

Boccuzzi, G. 2015. "Crediti in sofferenza e crisi bancarie." http://www.ipeistituto.it/master/images/file-pdf/convegni/GiuseppeBoccuzzi_Convegno11dicembre2015.pdf, (October 15, 2017 accessed).

Cribis D&B. 2017. "Payment Study 2017." https://www.dnb.ru/media/entry/54/Payment_Study_2017_Light.pdf (January 12, 2017 accessed).

Ernst and Young. 2016. "Asset-backed Securitization and Accounts Receivable Factoring Overview," *SFTMA Symposium*, www.ey.com/Publication/vwLUAssets/EY-asset-backed-securitization-and-accounts-receivable-factoring-overview/$FILE/EY-asset-backed-securitization-and-accounts-receivable-factoring-overview.pdf (October 15, 2016 accessed).

European Banking Authority, 2018. "Risk Dashboard Annex.Credit Risk parameters", fourth quarter, https://www.eba.europa.eu/documents/10180/2175405/KRI+-+Risk+parameters+annex+-+Q4+2017.pdf/727b2f01-75d0-45e9-9e37-2153f3fd3fe2, (May 20, 2018 accessed).

Factors Chain International. 2016. "Statistics." https://fci.nl/en/solutions/statistics2018, (September 11, 2017 accessed).

Intrum Justitia. 2017. "European Payment Report." www.intrum.com/press/publications/european-payment-report-2017/

Marketinvoice. 2017. "Learning Center." https://learn.marketinvoice.com/, (October 10, 2017 accessed).

United States Census. 2016. "Quarterly Financial Report." https://www.census.gov/econ/qfr/historic.html (May 22, 2017 accessed).

Websites

Bank for International Settlements, www.bis.org

Board of Governors of the Federal Reserve System, https://www.federalreserve.gov/

Bureau of Economic Analysis, Department of Commerce, https://www.bea.gov/

Cribis D&B, www.dnb.com

Ernst & Young, www.ey.com

Factors Chain International (FCI), https://fci.nl/en/home

Italian Factoring Association (ASSIFACT), www.assifact.it

U.S. Census Bureau, https://www.census.gov/

World Bank, www.worldbank.org

Annex

Table A.1 Sectorial branches description

Code	Description
051	Products of agriculture, forestry, and fishing
052	Energy products
053	Minerals and ferrous and nonferrous metals excluding fissile and fertile metals
054	Minerals and products based on nonmetallic minerals
055	Chemical products
056	Metal products, excluding machines and means of transport
057	Agricultural and industrial machines
058	Office machines, data processing machines, high-precision and optical instruments
059	Electrical material and supplies
060	Transportation vehicles
061	Food, beverages, and tobacco products
062	Textile products, leather and footwear, clothing
063	Paper, paper goods, newspapers, and publishing
064	Rubber and plastic products
065	Other industrial products
066	Building and public works
067	Trade
068	Hotels and other public services
069	Transportation services
070	Maritime and air transportation services
071	Services to transportation
072	Communication services
073	Other trade services

About the Author

Lucia Gibilaro is associate professor in economics of financial intermediaries at the University of Bergamo and visiting professor at the Athens University of Economics and Business. She obtained her master's in asset management and PhD in banking and finance from the University of Rome "Tor Vergata." She has been visiting scholar at the University of Essex. She is a member of the research center CISAlpino Institute of Comparative Studies in Europe at the University of Bergamo and she collaborates with the Real Estate Finance Laboratory at the University of Rome "Tor Vergata." She is the author of publications on asset-based lending, risk management, and fintech.

Index

OTHER TITLES IN OUR FINANCE AND FINANCIAL MANAGEMENT COLLECTION

John A. Doukas, Old Dominion University, *Editor*

- *Global Mergers and Acquisitions, Second Edition: Combining Companies Across Borders, Volume I* by Abdol S. Soofi and Yuqin Zhang
- *Global Mergers and Acquisitions, Second Edition: Combining Companies Across Borders, Volume II* by Abdol S. Soofi
- *Risk and Win!: A Simple Guide to Managing Risks in Small and Medium-Sized Organizations* by John Harvey Murray
- *Essentials of Financial Risk Management: Practical Concepts for the General Manager* by Rick Nason and Brendan Chard
- *Essentials of Enterprise Risk Management: Practical Concepts of ERM for General* Managers by Rick Nason and Leslie Ieming
- *Frontiers of Risk Management, Volume I: Key Issues and Solutions* by Dennis Cox
- *Frontiers of Risk Management, Volume II: Key Issues and Solutions* by Dennis Cox
- *The Art and Science of Financial Modeling* by Anurag Singal
- *Escape from the Central Bank Trap, Second Edition: How to Escape From the $20 Trillion Monetary Expansion Unharmed* by Daniel Lacalle
- *Mastering Options: Effective and Profitable Strategies for Traders* by Philip Cooper
- *Understanding Cryptocurrencies: The Money of the Future* by Arvind Matharu

Announcing the Business Expert Press Digital Library

Concise e-books business students need for classroom and research

This book can also be purchased in an e-book collection by your library as

- a one-time purchase,
- that is owned forever,
- allows for simultaneous readers,
- has no restrictions on printing, and
- can be downloaded as PDFs from within the library community.

Our digital library collections are a great solution to beat the rising cost of textbooks. E-books can be loaded into their course management systems or onto students' e-book readers.
The **Business Expert Press** digital libraries are very affordable, with no obligation to buy in future years. For more information, please visit **www.businessexpertpress.com/librarians**.
To set up a trial in the United States, please email **sales@businessexpertpress.com**.

www.ingramcontent.com/pod-product-compliance
Lightning Source LLC
Chambersburg PA
CBHW071841200326
41519CB00016B/4189